WHERE WAS I?

# Also by Stephen Kessler

POETRY

*Scratch Pegasus* 2013
*Burning Daylight* 2007
*Tell It to the Rabbis* 2001
*After Modigliani* 2000
*Living Expenses* 1980
*Beauty Fatigue* 1978
*Thirteen Ways of Deranging an Angel* 1977
*Poem to Walt Disney* 1976
*Nostalgia of the Fortuneteller* 1975

TRANSLATION

*Reality and Desire* (poems by Luis Cernuda) 2015
*Poems of Consummation* (poems by Vicente Aleixandre) 2013
*Desolation of the Chimera* (poems by Luis Cernuda) 2009
*Eyeseas* (poems by Raymond Queneau, translated with Daniela Hurezanu) 2008
*Written in Water* (prose poems by Luis Cernuda) 2004
*Aphorisms* (prose by César Vallejo) 2002
*Heights of Machu Picchu* (poem by Pablo Neruda) 2001
*Ode to Typography* (poem by Pablo Neruda) 1998
*Save Twilight* (poems by Julio Cortázar) 1997
*From Beirut* (poem by Mahmoud Darwish) 1992
*Akrílica* (poems by Juan Felipe Herrera, translated with Sesshu Foster) 1989
*The Funhouse* (novel by Fernando Alegría) 1986
*Changing Centuries* (poems by Fernando Alegría) 1985
*Widows* (novel by Ariel Dorfman) 1983
*Homage to Neruda* (poems by eight Chilean poets) 1978
*Destruction or Love* (poems by Vicente Aleixandre) 1976

FICTION

*The Mental Traveler* (novel) 2009

NONFICTION

*Need I Say More? Portraits, Confessions, Reflections* (essays) 2015
*The Tolstoy of the Zulus: On Culture, Arts & Letters* (essays) 2011
*Moving Targets: On Poets, Poetry & Translation* (essays) 2008

EDITOR

*The Sonnets* by Jorge Luis Borges 2010

*Where Was I?*

STEPHEN KESSLER

Greenhouse Review Press

Copyright © 2015 by Stephen Kessler

All rights reserved. No portion of this book may be reproduced or transmitted in any form or by any means, electronic or mechanical, including photocopying and recording, or by any information storage or retrieval system, without permission in writing from Greenhouse Review Press, except in brief quotations used in articles or reviews.

Greenhouse Review Press
3965 Bonny Doon Road
Santa Cruz, CA 95060

Designed by Gary Young

ISBN 978-0-9838094-0-1

Manufactured in the United States of America

Distributed by Small Press Distribution (spdbooks.org)

*for Traci Hukill*

ACKNOWLEDGMENTS

Grateful acknowledgment is due to the editors of *Cerise Press, Chicago Quarterly Review, 5_trope, Good Times, Hilltromper, Miramar, Or, phren-Z, Red Wheelbarrow, The Redwood Coast Review,* and *Santa Cruz Weekly,* where many of these pieces, some in earlier versions, originally appeared.

"Tor House, Carmel" was published as a limited edition photographic broadside by Catamaran Literary Reader.

For their friendship and critical encouragement of these writings the author wishes to thank Traci Hukill, Walter Martin, Carolyn Tipton, Marc Hofstadter, Rebecca Taksel, Barry Fruchter, Roger Greenwald, Kay Bradner, Robert Sward, Lucas Lackner, Joseph Matthews, Gary Young, and Alta Ifland.

# Contents

Senior Discount    13
A Bike Ride on the Westside    14
State Route One    15
A Night at the Civic    16
My Dream Library    17
Camden Drive    18
The Gypsy Wagon    19
Spanish Steps    20
Doris Avenue    21
Downtown Africa    22
A Clean, Dimly Lit Place    23
At Groucho's House    24
The *Zvir*    25
The Lilly    26
Café Life    27
State Street    28
Not Far from the Tar Pits    29
Down the Road    30
Unread Books    31
Happy Hour in Fort Bragg    32
A Supermarket in California    33
A Classic Example    34
Santa Anita    35
Photography Exhibition    36
Centro Sol    37
Ice Cream Grade    38
Green Monk    39
A Spanish Mansion    40
The Record    41

Roxbury Park    42
Tor House, Carmel    43
Early Girls    44
Unchained Buddha    45
Midnight in Santa Cruz    46
Facing West from California's Shores    47
*Terroirisme,* or Proust at the Wine Bar    48
Mission Street    49
Barrio Santa Cruz    50
Little Dume    51
Shades of Lady Day    52
Post Office    53
Inside *The Sun*    54
Near Broadway and Columbus    55
Old Standards    56
Rites of Night    57
Neighborhood Watch    58
Live Music at Moe's Alley    59
Summer Travelers    60
Riverside Drive    61
Younglove Avenue    62
Office Hours    63
Coyoacán    64
Car Wash    65
Davenport Roadhouse    66
Silver Lake    67
Loring and Wyton    68
Hoover Road    69
A Walk on the Wharf    70

Central Park   71
Pensión Las Once   72
The Floating World   73
Farmers Market   74
West Cliff Blues Again   75
Failed Recluse   76
A Day in LA   77
Hours in Logos   78
On the 101   79
Having Sex in Mexico with Cernuda   80
Too Much, Too Late   81
Marriott Courtyard, Culver City   82
Boardwalk Odyssey   83
Air Cubana   84
Village Vanguard   85
Wine Country   86
From the Front Deck   87
Sunset Boulevard   88
Dream Museum   89

# *Where Was I?*

Different places on the face of the earth have different vital effluence, different vibration, different chemical exhalation, different polarity with different stars: call it what you like. But the spirit of place is a great reality.

—D. H. Lawrence, *Studies in Classic American Literature*

# Senior Discount

In some way you are diminished, and so these businesses—the moviehouse, the grocery, the Goodwill, the discount store that already slashes prices—knock a percentage off your purchases as a gesture of compassion for your shrunken condition. You don't exactly *feel* old, unless you happen to notice your wizened visage in the mirror or the pain in your joints or the ancient habits you repeat as if in perpetuity, but you know you are. You see pierced babes and tattooed dudes in the sexual heat of early summer shedding that warmth in waves as they walk entwined on Front Street, and know in your bones from a long way off exactly that romance in retrospect, an old-school honor roll of remembered loves, each eternal in its moment, every one always lost somehow, even the one you married, because you're driven like gulls by a stiff wind or kelp in surf tumbling into oblivion, with art your only flotation device, if briefly, before a tsunami of devastating abstractions—time, history, transience, change—up and wipes you out. That's why it's cheaper to watch a film, or buy that secondhand shirt on Tuesdays, or that basket of fresh figs you will taste intensely as if for the last time. Even if your mother lived to be ninety-four and your dad only died at seventy-five because of those big dark cigars he smoked, and half your aunts and uncles put up an epic fight, you're doomed, get used to it, and while you're at it enjoy these warming days between natural and man-made disasters when the mild sky swears it will stay sunny and the air carries currents of birdsong and honeysuckle, and though you seem to be losing friends in a plague of irreversible disappearances, you are more present than ever, tasting twilight like a dry white wine with a crisp yet paradoxically endless finish. You're acutely aware of the creamy flowers in the magnolia across the street, and the fog in its slow cool takeover of the bay, and the zephyr caressing your neck like some phantom hand.

# A Bike Ride on the Westside

The bike cost twenty bucks at the Goodwill, what timing to find it, what a deal, it's white with rusty spokes, it works, it fits, and so you take your aging heart for a spin, sunlight revealing a long view across the bay, and now you are turning a corner downhill letting gravity have its way with you and your wheels one late afternoon in April, breeze in your helmet, subtle joy in the soul to be gliding so easily along through such hard times, pushing across Mission with the signal and getting a whiff of the pizza place yielding to vapors venting from the Laundromat then a trace of something frying in grease and garlic from the Chinese diner, a rush of smells pulling primal recall in different directions, but before you can do a Proust you are sailing down Swift across the railroad tracks which jolt you back to the present past the lavender bushes and then the acreage under construction on Delaware before you turn toward Natural Bridges and cruise past the beautiful eucs, their extravagant smell like your love's wild hair where butterflies light in May, bright wings drinking the warmth of sunlight, but not just yet, this sun is cool, and as it slants west you zoom down into the gulch and pump back up toward the beach, and soon you're there, on West Cliff, breathing the briny, iodine-rich, foam-sprayed coastal view including the wave lovers riding the swells and women out for their evening run whose scent you catch for a flash and elderly couples savoring a walk and men with dogs and young girls gossiping and guys in parked trucks gazing out to sea and clusters of kids passing a joint whose sweet smoke gives you a slight lift as you head for the lighthouse wondering how such simple luck as this can exist, it must be some kind of dream where you turn a corner and the bay curves too, revealing a vision of fabulous forms on a boardwalk next to the beach, and beyond, a little city that looks almost mythical snuggling up to its hills.

# State Route One

In Malibu they call it the Pacific Coast Highway along where the canyons cut their way to the bay, or beyond Point Dume to the ocean, and either way the fires rage down through the chaparral every few years, sometimes all the way to this wide road protecting expensive coastside homes from random razings. In Big Sur they call it the Coast Road and its cliffs invite scenic suicides as the wrecks rusting in the rocky surf attest. As Cabrillo Highway heading toward the City past Pigeon Point it has an agricultural air as the fields on both sides testify, strawberries and Brussels sprouts establishing delicious dialectics for the tourists who race past toward some tasty restaurant, and for the locals headed for the farmers markets. Across the Golden Gate it enters legend, not just of the jumpers in one last act of exhilaration, but of architecture itself, the gracefully engineered gateway to Point Reyes, through bohemian Bolinas and up through Bodega Bay to Shoreline Highway where raptors cruise in search of prey and you can glimpse them for a split second but no longer lest you plunge over the edge or slam into some log truck coming back from whacking the landscape. Late at night I've seen mountain lions, swerved around skunks that stepped in front of my headlights, thought about lots of things in the long dark drive home to a cold house and a heart in ruins. But on this road, home is the whole unrolled dark ribbon of it up and down the coast where your whole life has unfolded in so many cars with all those loves alongside, or solo as the day is long as you drove to or from some loss or other, some face you've all but forgotten in the sweet shade of a summer afternoon so beautifully in reach of the creamy breakers that rolled in foaming as you rolled by at the limit. And these passings are permanent even as the highway is, whatever slides or slipouts have closed it in winter storms, there's a way around and you keep going.

# A Night at the Civic

The library book-sale tables are out of sight, the basketball backboards stashed backstage and the Roller Derby track rolled up in a storeroom somewhere. Folding chairs stand in straight rows as the jazzophiles file in and find their seats, anxious to hear the men in matching suits from New York blow into town and blow the town down, their Ellingtonian lungs deployed to raze this gym with a sound as powerful as Willie Mays. The band struts in from the wings, sits, and starts blowing Dukelike from sheet music, the brass muted so it almost squeaks from the trombonists' noses, fast, with a classical tone, a hard Boppishness wrapped in uptown tailoring that morphs into a light blue Monkdom, tooting a little ironically along with graver accents of deep lefthanded melancholy. Such changes, harmonized in the same time, are simultaneous and, in what could otherwise be redundant, establish a repeating pattern that sings in a most distinctive way. Now the trumpets take off the gloves and start making a sound like avian invaders, those strange birds that fly up your ears and soar in the stunned brain. Wild, these mating calls, like those of vocalists in love arguing, loud and oddly melodic, almost Dizzy in their flippant lucidity. The players are sweating under their silk suits as the bus rolls into New Orleans on a hot night, one tire busted so as to create a complex syncopation, churchy and funky, sultry in the way of cool *mulatas* with fruit on their hats, blatantly dangerous, the last of their kind since cigarettes are taboo and the mint in your julep could be bugged. Because *everything is listening.* The trees on Walnut Avenue are catching the day's last rays and trembling a little, trying to shake off the shadows. If you put your ear to the train tracks running down Chestnut you can hear the saxophones in the front row, I swear, speaking Swahili. The sky darkens and Monday night settles over the lighthouse. The moon is smiling as it rises behind the mountains, and seems to swing.

# My Dream Library

It's downtown but it's in the mountains. It has no computers but there's a full bar (the bartenders double as librarians). The walls are solid books except for the plate glass facing the redwood groves. Late last night, or was it early this morning, they were serving Akhmatova gimlets while a chanteuse was scatting a remarkably long riff of Dewey decimals and the librarian setting my drink on the brass bar winked at me from behind her designer frames as if we knew something no one else did about the volumes arrayed in rows all around and the view into the trees where she hinted we had once rendezvoused to read Rilke and contemplate the ways memories replace romance as we age. This place is a refuge at all hours, a shelter for those with no place else to go, and there's always entertainment, dead or alive, all these pages teeming with evidence of lost and found existences, and the performers somehow tap into your mood and seem to be attuned to how blue or green or pink or purple you feel and echo that tone in whatever they're playing. The barkeeps recommend books—no bestsellers—and through the skylight mural overhead the stars are visible, or mythic clouds full of gods, or a golden radiance. Wirelessly we are connected here to so many immortals it is dizzying to consider we inhabit the same world. I ask with my eyes across the circulation desk if you'll meet me in the stacks so we can compare our readings of *Women in Love* but you pretend you don't notice, leaving me to imagine our intelligent conversation, which only intensifies my desire. Heard melodies are sweet, but unheard, nobody knows the difference. These nights and days on the last barricades before paper is obsolete have the intense flavor of our final kiss, when we could savor Paradise disappearing. That's why I'm nursing this drink, the long sips of this book, your face, trying to hold in the mind what we read together those eternal evenings, taste whatever your tongue was trying to tell me.

# Camden Drive

The magnolias have grown, now casting much more gorgeous and generous shade; my house is gone, its stately historic scale replaced by modern monstrosities bulging off their lots; and the street seems quieter from here with its few but costly cars and hardly any kids on bikes. Rodeo Drive has lost its horse path long ago and descends into luxury shops and galleries where hardware stores and haberdashers were. The streetcar line on Santa Monica is gone, as is Gramps who rode with me to Hollywood matinees, yet cops who cruised these drives still make their regular rounds to protect the residents from unpredictable eruptions of desperate bums. Why am I here? I fled this neighborhood ages ago, had to get out and grow up, yet I return because its smells—those creamy blossoms breathing between those dark green gleaming leaves—are perennial, like the gardening crews that keep the yards under control and smelling of mown grass. Out of a long driveway no longer there one of my brother's friends backs up his car and flattens a kitten, and to prove how tough they are they all laugh at the corpse displayed on a badminton racquet. We are so far from there, and from the front-yard football games where we tried to dodge the dog shit and the sprinkler heads, and some of those kids are dead by now, and the rest old, yet all is as possessed as it is lost, or possesses us, unpredictably, like the Flexy we sped down the sidewalk on like a bobsledder. We were charmed then as we are still with gifts of good luck that kept us alive so we look back even as we sit half a century away on some other steps and relive what we missed the first time. What we were heading into was a world of greater and greater bewilderment even as we learned to navigate it, so much more complicated than these seemingly calm rectangles of land. The lights at night behind closed windows sometimes spoke of domestic dramas too mundane, too tragic to imagine.

# The Gypsy Wagon

Those greasy burgers behind the Humanities building were fuel for philosophical conversations, our elbows on the picnic table and our mouths chewing and talking about Kierkegaard or Hopkins' "Wreck of the Deutschland" with all those nuns going down and a sound unlike anything we'd ever known. We were barely nineteen, or you were maybe twenty, and we knew almost nothing or just enough to get us started, and those books were like explosives in our brains, and some of our professors were provocateurs recruiting us into dangerous undertakings, pages and pages of occult instructions and understandings through which we came to unknow our own families and instead felt bound by blood to writers we'd never met who seemed to read our minds and speak of the same miseries and mysteries tormenting us, and so when we'd meet after class to eat and debrief on Blake or Sophocles under the trees by the trailer where the burgers were being flipped and the sodas jerked from the taps, we were beside ourselves with revelations no less astounding for being sophomoric. We were surrounded by beautiful girls, or we were so hungry for beauty they looked that way as they walked and looked past us, and that was okay because we were Transcendentalists, or Existentialists, or beatniks in training though we didn't know it, trying to transcend our upbringings without any notion of what for, trying to exist for no reason we could fathom. We were skinny and wiry, with pimples, with unformed longings, with desires absent appropriate objects, and with appetites attached for now to those soft buns dripping with pickles and mustard and drops of grease from the grill. How could we have imagined then that you would grow a beard and a big belly and become rabbinical, and I would become someone who sits at a sidewalk café and watches miscellaneous pedestrians stroll past in Mediterranean weather at the solstice, and records such sightings for their own sake as he invokes or tries to recover moments close to half a century removed that he all but didn't notice at the time.

# Spanish Steps

Keats's flat in Rome was a little tight for my taste but he was even more of a shrimp than me, and he'd gone there to die, after all, so all he needed was a comfortable bed and a friend to help him through the fever beforehand. But just outside the door, even then, if a little less busy than when I was there in sixty-six and a lot less swarming with tourists than now, lovers were surely smooching and couples strolling and vendors displaying their stuff in the Italian sun, water spilling deliberately in fountains to imitate the sound of mountain streams, so everything he needed was there except the one he adored and hoped to return to but it was too late, he was whistling in the dark past the graveyard where his name would soon be writ in water in stone and young poets would make pilgrimage to meditate over his bones. I did that one time, haunted his rooms then went to the cemetery to stare at the stone, maybe on the same afternoon. Such voyeuristic hungers have made me track phantoms into the farthest reaches of their fame and consume them so as to assume, like some mad scientist, their poultergasms completely and be filled with the bitter juice of their genius and hope it would stick and not just be excreted the next day. I would profane almost anyone in order to taste what they knew and make it into something I could use without shame in the marketplace of disgrace and be hung out to dry in the stocks and be stared at by passing kids and glared at embarrassedly by their parents for having performed unspeakable acts of transubstantiation in a public place, disgusting. But when you're dying and had never got together with your girlfriend what else can you do but try to breathe and be inspired by whatever you can even if it means traveling and landing in a room you never imagined in order to say one final goodbye to the show just on the other side of the wall.

# Doris Avenue

That tiny street was just uphill from the treatment plant and a short hike from the beach, which we could smell sometimes and almost see from the back deck of our cottage as we tried as best we could to settle into the first terrors of marriage, of being adults, of making love not war but also making war without knowing better or much of anything else, and it hurt to be so stupid but we were young, and the highway patrolman across the street who parked his cruiser there while home for lunch made matters worse, we were paranoid enough already as we smoked the slim joints you rolled in your long, skilled fingers. I wanted to be a poet and spent hours at the machine, its electric hammers rattling echoes off the sheetrock walls of my office as I typed and ripped and revised and typed again, wrestling a few thin lines into an order I hoped would be true, and the handsome stray cat who adopted us was like a muse to me, poetry on paws. The baseboard heating was worthless and the ceiling lacked insulation, so it was cold at night and we burned whatever we could in the sheetmetal fireplace, which could be stoked to a glow that we were lucky didn't burn down the house. I almost felt as if I had a job, commuting to classes like a little professor in training, but I couldn't take it, nor being bound to you, because after the brief relief of our sex there was nothing for us to do but be afraid—chaos reigned—the country was coming apart and we'd have brought it down if we could, but for all our hair we were merely kids from the tamest part of LA. And so time did with us what it does with any of its young: it flung us ruthlessly into a spooky future. That little rental in Rio Del Mar was a place where we were seduced and deluded by the greenest hopes, yet somehow we endured the disaster and lived to survive our love and become ourselves.

# Downtown Africa

This is where music started, Eve and Adam listening to insects and breezes in the grasses, moonlight obscured by rainclouds and then lightning, rumbling drums or a pianist's heavy left hand laying down a bass line for a black saxophone sounding across the savannah and fast cats chasing down their prey who cry plaintively, briefly, as they are eaten, harmonizing with the brutality of being, a link in the chain and honored to be devoured. All this occurs a great distance from its origins because how else could you be somewhere you never were otherwise, musicians your only means of transport, and they are efficient, a few strokes of the fingertips, a few breaths and you are aloft as if atop an elephant, the rhythm of its walk rocking you while its trunk swings in distinct syncopation and its little tail sways lightly behind, the veldt unfolding ahead of you and jungle all around beyond, birds rowing overhead and calling out the names of their destinations, creating an itinerary as they fly. Here you have no guide but sound itself, no Land Rover, no tent to protect you and so you must watch your step in the dark lest you stumble over a sleeping lion or over a big snake moving so beautifully it makes a sinuous sound on the ground like the voice of temptation itself encouraging you to taste what tells you more than you need to know, not in language exactly but in the texture of understanding on the tongue when it touches its double in a beloved mouth. Out of the sky falls a newspaper to ruin everything, a world of pain in print to tell lovers how lucky they are. It was always thus, Paradise interruptus, then loss, bewilderment, regret, memory, the sense that if only the kisses had been more articulate it would have turned out differently when in fact the bad news would have come down anyway and you must live tragically ever after, if even that, if you didn't die of bliss in the first place. And if you listen, this is where your pulse comes from.

# A Clean, Dimly Lit Place

After the movie, late at night, when the spouse is away and there's no place to go but home nor any reason to, you like to retreat to a certain restaurant steps from the bay where the Aztec Zen feng shui is serene and the margaritas reliably brisk and limey. Here, in the amber light and deep green walls, with one candle burning low inside the table lamp, you can sit in a corner with the pleasing sting of salsa on your tongue and sip your drink and write as if there were something still to say about the end of May in a drizzly spring, or Memorial Day in the fog of several wars, or the bay with its waves and their curling white smiles and the passing whales whose curves and white spouts break the surface barely a baseball's throw beyond the breaking surf. That light—tinged blue, blue-gray or steely silver above the pelican squadrons cruising so gracefully ungainly, and over the flocks of wetsuited humans floating in search of an eternal break—reflects with generosity on everything, or so it seems those afternoons in the glint of one long breezily sunlit look. Even from here, at night, in the red-chile light and the gleam of the *vino del día* and the frosty glow of gold *cervezas* on adjacent tables, conversations creating a suggestive buzz for muses on the alert for some stray word, you can almost understand the water rocking in the dark in the near distance, whispering salty nothings into your hungry ears. "I eat with my eyes," says the cheerfully starving artist whose thinness gives him an angle of vision keen enough to see everything, sharply, but now your plate has arrived. The Spanish love songs crooned as if forever with their kitschy lyrics reassure somehow that nothing will change, that you will remain suspended where time can't touch you. This must be the purpose of such a place, an oasis, a kind of home where nothing is yours and you don't care. Because all that counts is now.

# At Groucho's House

When I was a student at Beverly Hills High way back in the last century I had a reputation for dating every cute girl I could find. "Kessler will go out with anyone who'll kiss him," one of my so-called friends once said behind my back. It's true, what can I say, and what after all is wrong with wanting to kiss as many cute teenage girls as possible? Anyway, one of the cutest girls in my class was Melinda Marx, daughter of Groucho. She had pale skin and dark eyes and thick dark hair and was slim and little, like me, and she seemed kind of shy and sweet, so I asked her out. She lived in Truesdale Estates, a new development in the hills just west of West Hollywood; most of the lots had sleek midcentury modern houses with spectacular views of LA, at night especially, when the lights shone up through the smog and spread in an endless grid all the way to the ocean. It was a Friday night when I went to pick up Melinda. I rang the bell and was invited in and stepped down into the living room where sheets of plate glass revealed the vast city below. Her father, Groucho himself, emerged from another room and she introduced us. He greeted and dismissed me perfunctorily, as if to say *Nice to meet you, kid, now get out of here.* (He wasn't smoking a cigar and he didn't say anything funny, like *Pull down your pants, kid, and let's see if you've got any balls.*) I think our curfew was midnight. We probably went to dinner and a movie. Our date, alas, was less than memorable. Melinda was not very talkative or witty or interesting or interested in me. In conversation—whatever sixteen-year-olds could have to say—her cuteness was somehow diminished. Groucho's daughter, oddly enough, struck me as rather dull. And her dad was decidedly grouchy. We didn't make out in front of that fabulous view, and I honestly can't recall if we even kissed.

# The *Zvir*

Belowdecks with the crew in my bachelor's bunk underneath Richard the gay guy from New York, I caught lice from the pleasantly rough sheets, or so I discovered by the time we landed in Casablanca. It was a long crossing, with several stops in East Coast ports to load freight, and there was time to get to know the crew a little and learn to toast in Serbo-Croatian, *Zhivili!* Every evening after the first-class passengers had finished dinner, Zvonka the cabin boy strode to the stern with a bucket of waste and dumped it overboard, enriching the Atlantic with food and trash for the fish, just as those twin spinsters from the Midwest were doing their brisk laps around the deck as if that could be a cure for constipation. I kept on reading the copy of *Anna Karenina* I'd found in the ship's library; her breasts were heaving in the ballroom just as the vessel was riding the swells and I could tell she was doomed from the first dance but I read on because what else was there to do out there with nothing but ocean in every direction as if forever. I was bound for Spain, I was thirty-one, I had an appointment in Madrid with the Nobel laureate, who was my friend because I'd translated his book and he was grateful, and on the way I would stay in his native Andalucía. From here in Half Moon Bay thirty-five years on it feels like a dream, a myth of imagined glory, but it was true, a poet's actual journey into legend, with parasites in his pubic hair to prove it. This was Romance writ large, the itching was evidence, as was the room with the bare bulb hanging from a wire in the middle of the ceiling in the cheap pensión in Algeciras where the potion from the pharmacy burned my balls in the shower as it killed the crabs. This too was poetry and I was lucky to be young and alive after so many days aboard that freighter whose flag was of a country that doesn't exist anymore.

# The Lilly

This is where my archives are, a seven-story bunker, most of it underground, built by a pharmaceutical fortune to withstand the tornadoes of Indiana. Anyone can walk in and ask to rummage through my papers, and someone on the staff will fetch them and the visiting scholar or former lover will spread them out to read, as if that will tell them anything important. They—you—may even be reading this very ink I'm laying down on this one and only page, there in a time and place beyond my reach, as if what I'm doing is an act of faith in an afterlife. Three floors down on a shelf near Sylvia Plath's schoolgirl letters, or William Carlos Williams's collected postcards, or Ezra Pound's annotated *Playboy*s (or whatever he marginalized), some papers of mine may be fluttering in eternity, or in the oblivion of memory perpetually unlooked-up, the mountains of manuscripts untouched by biographers busy chasing more famous phantoms. And so these pages may remain unscanned by human eyes, though anyone with a modem can read the catalog and see the miles of items that testify on my behalf even if no one calls them to the witness stand. How odd to exist on paper alone—though no worse than in some computer—speaking to someone I don't know. Like all but a few of the library's collections, my stuff will sit there awaiting the tender hand that will reach and touch. Whatever and whoever I thought I was writing for or speaking to at the time will be as nonexistent as I am, and the unlikely researcher—in search of *what* exactly?—will, if he or she should ever exist, at least be alive, and we will be connected inexplicably, even if explication is the rationale. I'm dreaming of course that such lines as these might be thought significant enough to read, as if dead documents in climate-controlled stacks a couple of thousand miles from here, now quiet in the middle of the night, might, as in some horror movie, someday get up and walk, might even speak.

# Café Life

In the cool of the afternoon I am tapping my laptop among the other typists in this caffeinated oasis, the music not too painfully loud though even at this volume the techno-beat is tough on any intelligence, and my head is barely buzzed by the aroma of fresh espresso. The very sight of all these youths engaged with their tools suggests a human community and makes my aged analogous body feel more virtually alive, almost contemporary, ever present despite a sense of advancing obsolescence. Living is an act of imagination; the older you are, the more you have to imagine. Everything takes time, and time takes everything, and so you have to pay closer attention in order to retain in your mind's eye the Mohawk on the otherwise lovely head of the young barista whom you once happen to have picked up hitching a ride from campus, where you had been using the library, downtown to this very café where she was late for work. You must register and remember as much as you can because you are not Funes, plagued by the inability to forget, but rather an absentminded Romantic so busy being attuned to Beauty that you may neglect to notice the merely beautiful with which so many streets and rooms are subtly brimming. Even young men are beginning to get to me, physical echoes of a kind of music I can scarcely make anymore, or am I an echo of theirs, their keyboards clicking out code for scores of symphonic compositions of which they are unconscious because they are not the composers but the song. Under the thudding metronomic pulse the hearts of the clientele are also thumping, their blood pumping happily through elastic capillaries without their even being aware. I admire the room's clean lines and airy light and intelligent design with negative space to spare and therefore plenty of room for emptiness and nothingness to circulate. The customer lifting a foamy cappuccino off the counter and turning slowly in search of a seat might as well be Isadora Duncan, so easy she makes it look to embody grace.

# State Street

In Chicago, at the Embassy Suites on State Street, around the corner from the Redhead Piano Bar where you sipped a Fonseca ten-year tawny Port alone in a crowd that talked nonstop while the player performed a flickering assortment of torch songs, you were attending a conference with fateful consequences. It wasn't the hustlers on State who changed your life, nor the icy wind off the lake in late October, nor your colleagues talking about translation, but there was one with whom you struck up a conversation, and then you were in a group going to dinner, and from there to a club where everyone but you was dancing to those blues—and on the way back from the club, on a side street just a couple of blocks from State, on the sidewalk outside an apartment tower, there were people milling around, and police tape and cops and paramedics, and murmurs of how a woman had jumped to her death just minutes before, and that was so strange, it gave the night another dimension of unsustainable sorrow, and the festive group who had been dancing to the blues returned subdued to their tall hotel—and the next night there was jazz of screaming intensity, horns wailing angrily, beautifully, and she was beside you again, and all you were doing was listening, but you were alive, and the day after that she asked to see your hand, and traced the lines of your palm as if they could tell her something, and then she was rolling her luggage through the lobby and boarding a shuttle on State Street headed for O'Hare, and two years later you and she were married. State Street—it's almost generic, like Market or Main or Broadway, and it sounds as if it might mean nation or government, but no, to you it means state of grace, or art, or destiny, or melancholy intimately confessed as if to confirm a sad understanding, which makes the pleasures all the more persuasive, those little jolts of joy when eyes and language catch each other by chance and something happens you never would have imagined.

# Not Far from the Tar Pits

Women fifty feet long recline above the boulevard, their vast
skin advertising something beyond my means. Across from the
Ancient Mexico exhibit the taco trucks are parked to accommodate
museum patrons hungry for current culture. I sit near the tar pits
contemplating the gooey ooze still sticky after all these eons and
black as motor oil out of which rise mammoth skeletons ephemeral
as those blond monsters on the billboards whose beauty I've begun
to question. Finding a pen at Rite Aid may be more vitally useful than
chasing phantom embraces, though the classic love ballads of the
jazz station playing as you cruise are just as eternal as ever and the
after-lunch espresso in the bistro offers its own *frisson* of longing as
your pores absorb the warm air suffused with just enough emissions
to remind you where you are passing through again as if forever. You
drive as politely as possible but some of those with whom you share
the avenues have consumed more caffeine than you and are under
pressure. Even in the current transience of the moment you are fixed
on timelessness—trying to catch the courtesy of the postal clerk
and hold it beyond delivery of the bird-bedecked business envelope
or to record the smile of the waitress who brings the wine even so
early in the day—you are extemporaneous, outside time where there
is nothing to be done but notice. Later there may be margaritas or
mariposas or magdalenas or madeleines to proust your muses but
for now it is enough to sniff these tar pits for traces of their deathless
dinosaurs, immortal avatars of boyhood caught in recurrent cycles of
old ballparks, drive-ins, hamburger joints where the fries smell of lost
time and the sweet grease of the kitchen coats the sky with its original
oils. You must savor such artistic afternoons as if you've hiked the
wild hills of Dume near the walled compounds and steered your
Subaru through sinuous canyons and over dinner rescued pleasure
in the eyes of an old friend long unseen and equally surprised by the
day's gratuitous gifts.

# Down the Road

The Hergesheimer was a burger with bacon and grilled onions on greasy white toast, signature sandwich of Adolph's, the place down the road from campus where on Friday nights the kids who didn't head for the city hung out to drink and talk and listen to hits on the jukebox and sometimes dance or indulge their munchies. The ceiling was low and the light was mildly yellow and workingmen from Red Hook would drink at the bar while the college students partied. It was couple of miles from your room, and the drive down River Road was dangerous in the dark when the kids coming home were drunk or stoned or both, but it was the only place to go if you weren't hung up on finishing your work or you were done and had nothing else to do. Adolph and his wife, if I remember right, tended bar and there was a waitress, Ruth, who brought your drinks and food, and way in the back—unless that was someplace else, some other bar & grill—there was a pool table where your early practice allowed you to hold your own with the local hustlers, such as they were. Sometimes faculty would show up, Jean-Claude Barré my French teacher for example, who over beers one night mentioned the name Borges to me for the first time, or Annys Wilson whose husband Bill was my adviser and who told me how pointless it would be to try to write poems to please some imagined editor. But mostly it was your peers, the girls you were too shy to speak to, the aspiring-writer friends, the premature drunks and wasted heads with problems they were struggling to expunge. You knew almost nothing but you were hungry to understand, and you read books and wrote your papers on time, and smoked dope on the weekends after dark with dudes as clueless as you were, and you drove down the road with them to get a little more blasted when you had the chance. It was a roadside dive where nothing much happened worth the trouble to remember, and yet you do.

# Unread Books

I am surrounded by unread books. The library is mine, and so of course I have read some, perhaps quite a few, of these books. But I have spent most of my life, and many dollars, acquiring books that I have yet to read. Eventually I do read one or another of these books, one at a time, over time, as instinct or impulse or imperative demands. There is a deliciously deliberate randomness in such readings, and I am pleased to surprise myself with the selection and to discover, often, the rich existences resting patiently in piles of closed pages hinged on one side for the reader's convenience—mine—as I follow the argument or narrative or possibly lyric or ludic assortment of pieces that, added together and arranged, compose the book. And knowing of such existences oddly alive in the silence of the shut books makes the unread ones perfectly mysterious and enigmatic, like friends who have yet to reveal some stunning secret, or strangers in transit—say, on a train—before they tell you more than you thought possible. It is these, the unread ones, whose company I enjoy—ones that can't be downloaded from a cloud because I have no device, no application, no screen on which to disembody the beautiful spines and traveled covers I have likely cleaned because I bought them used and have rubbed gently with cotton and alcohol to remove the shmutz, the smudges and crusts of stains that may have stuck to the coated stock but can be expunged and disinfected with a few firm strokes before they are shelved and forgotten until remembered again, browsed, flipped through, perused, possibly even read from page one all the way through to the end. But meanwhile many remain unread, neglected, dusty with what has befallen them, that fine grit of time's glaze. I value their companionship; they promise pleasure and inspiration, consolation and illumination, and often enough boredom or exasperation, you never know until later, when you don't forget. They are like those unheard songs that figures on a Greek vase supposedly sing if you listen closely enough.

# Happy Hour in Fort Bragg

The moose head on the wall and the two-man saw tell me I'm not in LA anymore but deep in the heart of the Redwood Coast where the old mill is no more than a tourist attraction and the brewery the best place to hang while your pickup is being smogged for the DMV. You park yourself at the bar while both TVs sell sports and acne creams and you sip your Acme Pale Ale, brewed across the street on Route One and possibly pumped through underground pipes into the taps, the ocean an empty monument to itself just west beyond the abandoned lumber yard. A block beyond the old bowling alley, now called Calvary Church, and across from Denny's, Jennie's Giant Burgers issues aromas drawn from half a century since when you were a growing boy stopping after school for a bite at Biff's on Wilshire Boulevard, now highrised into oblivion like so many other Space Age establishments—Ship's, Dolores, even Hamburger Hamlet in bankruptcy last you heard—as time deletes what seemed indelible, just like the sawmill in this workingman's town slowly being turned bohemian. Look at yourself, hardly even an interloper yet a repeat offender as an editor, anomalously and unemployably intellectual, an underminer of illiteracy and an invisible pillar of local culture. The local color is a silvery green as demonstrated by those stands of eucalypts next to Jack's Muffler at the edge of town, and you are sworn to witness and report their beauty, unnoticed by the natives despite the trees' persistent display of their long leaves shining like a bride's hair in whatever light strikes them. These mild afternoons in early March when spring feels to have come a month too soon, you can only marvel at the strange patience it delivers, as if you could wait for anything in such a pause—even the arrival of your love long since missing and last seen in Chicago. See how the breeze conspires with a setting sun to give back all you thought lost as darkness rises and you down the last of your brew.

# A Supermarket in California

Across two streets from my old house just off Mission, with only U-Save Liquors in between, stood the sprawling monstrosity of the ancient Safeway, the Westside's sole supermarket, whose fluorescent glare could be experienced, with a certain psychic distress, deep after midnight when everything else was shut and you desperately needed a bottle of juice or a pint of ice cream that couldn't wait till morning. I was grateful then for that store's existence yet at the same time hated the hideousness of its terrible architecture, its gleaming pyramids of manufactured fruit and its endless aisles of tasteless packages and glaring colors of a night owl's nightmares. Spread out on a single story across a parking lot wasteland dotted with cars at any hour, it looked to be the size of a football field and dominated the neighborhood, where last week I rode by on my bike and found the store demolished, big Cats raking through the rubble with their steel claws, rats' nests of dead rebar piled in twisted heaps, mounds of smashed concrete waiting to be scooped up and hauled away—it reminded me of downtown after the earthquake, whole buildings deemed irreparably obsolete and taken down and carted off in block-long trucks leaving strange voids after the ruins. The Safeway building too was obsolete, not only ugly but forced finally out of the last century by competition from healthier companies marketing new dietary paradigms. The New Age organic grocery behemoths had forced sclerotic old Safeway to throw up a new store. So beyond the ruins of rubble behind the chain link protecting an about-to-be-born-again parking lot of even vaster acreage than before rises the newer, grander, even more monstrous Safeway, now open, with its café and deli and bakery and pharmacy fired up, and fresh designs on the discriminating shopper, more choices and bargain wars for all, more food than half of Africa consumes, while the old Safeway, scene of emergency munchies-relief and glaring predawn panic attacks, of mainstream shopping in a pre-organic epoch, is gone. I can almost mourn as I contemplate its remains.

# A Classic Example

Cooking dinner on a Wednesday night, I tune in public radio, actual airwaves, imagine that, not my private device with my private songs hermetically piped into my pre-programmed head, but unpredictable, possibly unfamiliar music streaming out of an antique boombox set on the counter, its antenna pulling in a sexy signal, violins guiding the rhythm of my chopping as the greens are prepared for the cast-iron skillet and an improvised omelet takes shape under my watchful hands and listening eyes. I know the DJ, his name is Dale; decades ago he delivered a load of kindling to my old farmhouse outside Soquel, a carload of cedar shingles torn off his house and about to start a winter's worth of fires in mine. How we are still alive these ages later I can't explain, but the sounds of his weekly show on KUSP reliably warm my kitchen as I stir the pasta into the boiling water or toss an *ensalada de la casa*. I relish hearing how news is overruled, Dvořák and Rodrigo testifying with strings to their passions transcending history, tragedy, language—melodies leaping and keeping time—or some pianist's fingers pronouncing sounds like the speech of nightingales, unrepeatable, because even though the notes are written and recorded, this moment is temporary, this garlic clove crushed uniquely under the knife blade, this onion's pungent crescents now sliced just so, this olive oil can only be poured this once while this Prokofiev sonata simmers in the background or a Schumann concerto shimmers like candles on an intimate table where some special occasion is celebrated. This must be how music nourishes, feeding us through the ears as we gaze in each other's eyes and taste what we've made over the years and in the presence of the present, its gift unwrapped on our plates to be savored as we are serenaded by a radio. I couldn't have foreseen the arrival of these sounds until the surprise of their streaming from the speakers into the heat of our appetites, nor could we have known these classical harmonies before we composed this meal.

# Santa Anita

The purple San Gabriels on a January day beyond the stables behind the backstretch were far more awesome than the lakes and flowers of Hollywood Park, even the Goose Girl with her exposed shoulders no match for those vertical mountains, and the Pasadena Freeway had primitive curves and ancient pavement, so the drive out seemed long, an adventure through old LA. Some early mornings when you went with your big brother to watch the workouts you could glimpse the horses up close and note how their delicate legs rose to haunches rippling with power even as they walked, and sprung from the starting gate later in the day the explosive force of their strength was something you've never felt anywhere else. Thoroughbreds, like the tall blondes strolling with the jockeys after the races when the two-dollar bettors slouched toward the parking lot leaving a trail of losing tickets littering the concrete floor of the grandstands, but all day they had hope, and your dad in his box was in his element smoking his Cuban cigars and shmoozing with the touts, *characters* he called them, a day at the track his Paradise regained, and yours those immortal hot dogs floating in dirty water to be slathered with mustard on a soft bun and savored from the second your front teeth popped the skin, tangy as anything you've ever tasted. The jockeys' glistening silks, the horses' flanks flashing as they came onto the track for the ritual parade before each race, the announcer's godlike voice, the murmur of thousands of horseplayers, and then the bell and the rumbling hooves and the mass yelling—what more could a boy want for excitement than to be with his dad on a Saturday afternoon chomping delicious franks and watching the beautiful animals through binoculars so as to engage the eyes in the glory of their bodies and their lovingly groomed coats. Driving home at day's end, the Andrews Sisters in the dashboard harmonizing a tune whose words you knew by heart, you could feel in your bones the echo of the crowd and the afterglow of the flying horses.

# Photography Exhibition

Vivian Maier, a Chicago nanny, took these pictures, so eloquently, anonymously, all through midcentury, leaving thousands of images unseen by anyone else while she was alive, discovered only later in a storage locker, sold at auction, and now displayed in an elite gallery. Fleeting eyes catch her art in passing, just as she caught the spirit of the city, click after click with exquisite timing, a face, two faces, a row of faces frozen in the heat of their shared humanity—such a frayed word after so much abuse but strangely beautiful with age, with wise tiredness after such years, such ages of solitude, like hers whose empathy mirrors them, her face reflected in shop windows holding her Rolleiflex waist high where it finds somehow the angle of soul in her acutely attuned eyes. As I resume my walkings I can almost begin to see the way the streets reach ever deeper into simple drama, so fraught, of every day and night—the lovers reunited over wine, a ghost of a chance flickering in the table's candle, chance of their ever having met, what a miracle, much less maintained their oneness. Was all this caught in those photos, her compassion for their passion, even if her own was never gratified? This French red begins to move my musings into a sphere not seen in the pictures, a zone of foreign emotion that feels impossibly real after barely a day on this island where white guys wearing black hats play tenor saxophones in dark basements to accompany old Romantics left to their own mnemonic devices whereby they remember everything lost and held always in the same breath, so many nights and mornings in the arms of her without whose wholly delivered heart its inspiration would be infinitely less. These thoughts are recorded in homage to one who saw the city in all its suffering glory, even its sidewalks, its buildings, its reaching bridges suffused with longing.

# Centro Sol

The afternoon you first arrived, in mid-July when everyone was gone and the rest of the city was taking a siesta, Madrid seemed asleep under its hot sun, though the iron balconies lining the buildings on calle Echegaray a few blocks from Puerta del Sol cast a filigree of geranium-scented shade over the cobblestones, and the young torero who appeared out of nowhere and asked if you were looking for postcards made you feel warmly welcomed. How many times since then have you walked those streets and sat in the Plaza Santa Ana adjacent to the classical teatros and in front of the Cervecería Alemana and two streets over from La Toscana where the kitchen masters as if eternally could be seen slicing tomatoes for the ensalada especial de la casa and at the next corner the tiled bar where gypsy kids could sing flamenco for a few pesetas, the whole barrio with its songs and its fried smells was music to your soul as you strolled in pursuit of poets who had hung out there forty years before. Reading the papers improved your Spanish, and having a few sangrías also helped you speak more fluently with the young gente you would meet by chance in the tabernas. People were on the street, on foot, having a drink and tapas after work, or smoking those cigarettes whose pungent smoke was a ravishing mixture of cancer and romance, because dying is part of living and the moment is to be savored in all its complex pleasures, its rich sensations, its wild talk and flirtations, like the woman who asked you what you were writing downstairs that night in the Cuevas del Sésamo and you didn't know what to tell her beyond the quote on the wall from Valéry: *Every kiss presages a new agony.* The black-clad widows could tell you that if you sat beside them on a bench and asked, but you were immersed in other wonders, like the pleasantly grimy side streets where ordinary pedestrians rushing along the sidewalks still had an aura of poetry forty years later.

# Ice Cream Grade

In summer the second-growth redwoods cooled things off and smelled good as the heat released aromas from their trunks, the forest floor, the branches sifting the bright light down in subtle dapplings, and the road's curves were sinuous as you crossed the creeks, and I wanted a house in the mountains and found one at the top of a long drive with a sharp switchback, a house I decided to buy, my first one, but the mountain was coming down around it because the road in had been graded without a permit at the foot of an ancient landslide, so after attempting to hold back the slope with retaining walls I had to sue the seller to take it back. That was how I met the lawyer from LA who hired a young hooker and brought her back to his suite at the Holiday Inn and while the charcoal was burning for the steaks he was about to broil in the fireplace she passed out, he told me the next morning over bacon and eggs at the Bubble Bakery. He had been Jim Morrison's lawyer after one bust or another, and told me I reminded him of Jim, young freaks who were sensitive poets under the hair. That road in the old days was the route between Bonny Doon and the ice cream socials on Empire Grade, and it felt primeval under those trees especially when it rained or at night when you came back from the saloon downtown where people got together to drink or listen to a local band or pick up someone to catch herpes from or otherwise take their chances in civilization. The redwoods were a refuge when they weren't a menace, offering shelter when their shallow roots weren't ripping loose in a storm and toppling onto your roof. I stayed in that house just a few months, never even moved in, the first big deal I'd ever made and it was doomed, and being in those dense woods in the dark was deeply unsettling, but forty years on a lot of people have built fancy homes up there.

# Green Monk

A drizzly Thursday thrashed by some bad gusts and downpours but calming down as the sun goes down and gray clouds grow dark over downtown where a young medium with a tight quartet is channeling Thelonious, just what I needed, a monastic reminder that a slight madness can be insanely sane, cracked with contagious syncopation that's sophisticated like a big city with its dark lights and bright darknesses, its red streaks creating loud traffic that stops and starts, sort of honks like black and white swans or ducks, dances in sound, until the power lines and the piano strings can hardly be told apart. I celebrate the rain by taking my muse to hear a few blue notes she can groove to, an absurd beauty not unlike Beckett, a let us say philosophical angle on melody, a bit offbeat, slightly cubist, subtly ironical, a tone of puzzlement and wonder at the pervasive strangeness. Empty storefronts recede into abstraction, mere economics, while here we gather in transcendence, a sanctuary of improvisation, temple of cool communion, mosque of unspeakable gods more powerful than movies or computers, their wonders wordlessly, uselessly gorgeous like all those non-native eucalypts festooning the surprised landscape with their silvery-green leaves. Have I forgotten anything—that dark green smell filling the farmers market? The light green honeysuckle tricked by a fake spring into shedding its scent above the recycling bins? The green-eyed cats that use the hill behind our house for a hunting ground? The one time I saw Monk and heard him alive he was so stoned or zoned out he just sat there nodding at the piano, maybe banging out a chord now and again but mostly just keeping the beat in some inner space only he could navigate. His sound is singular, inimitable, invented within a sphere of deep genius, one of a kind. Now again he can be heard and the sky is sobbing in response after all those warm sunny days, reservoirs filling and the city's gutters running, storm drains flowing to the ocean rhythmical as rivers.

# A Spanish Mansion

The Zen master was staying in the empty mansion that belonged to the precocious entrepreneur, and my ex and her partner were staying in the guest house (the Zen master was their teacher too) and she was having a psychotic break, which they were treating there with a circle of friends instead of sending her to the hospital. I was living with my love in New York but we happened to be traveling in California, and my ex called my best friend in San Francisco looking for me, so I got the message and called back and we drove down the Peninsula that afternoon and found the beautiful empty Spanish mansion, its huge rooms echoing with the silence of the tiles and the big beams and the wrought iron and the dark wood floor, one armchair with a floor lamp where the owner read, but he was nowhere to be seen. (I didn't know then that he would become a legend and that his business vision would change the world.) My ex was in the garden naked reading Walt Whitman and started reciting "Song of Myself" when she saw me coming, and my newer love was waiting in the car, I guess the situation was just too strange, she didn't understand that I could ever have loved anyone else, and maybe she was afraid of catching the madness. My ex was suffering, I could see that, she was agitated and misquoting Whitman, but all I could do was listen, be cool, try not to get infected with her mania. I went inside to ask the Zen master how he thought she was doing, but his redheaded wife protected him from having to deal with a stranger. I could see his back at the kitchen sink, but he never turned around. Perhaps the psychosis had freaked him out and the teacher had retreated into himself. It was a gorgeous house that has since been torn down to make way for something no doubt more monstrous, and some years later the Zen master drowned, and now the young man whose home it was is also gone.

# The Record

The record becomes increasingly random, jumping from book to book as the spirit moves, with no agenda but to soothe the mood of the savage geezer increasingly plagued by what he's losing, whole deserts and beaches of lovely sand slipping through his creaky fingers. Get a grip, he tries to tell himself, but he scarcely speaks his own language—maybe that's why he has to write for an ideal reader who understands—and those sands keep running waterwise through his lines of least resistance, unable to withstand the least passing passion without feeling the force of its sweet grief. So many poems he can't read, can't stand to hear at the mass gatherings or sad support groups of the earnest with nothing more useful to do than applaud one another's pathetic efforts. And who are you but one of them all your life in need of the same affirmation, trying to get their attention, or someone's, by singing into the wind. It's deaf, you know by now, or at least indifferent, as are the gatekeepers who send regrets that those lines lose something in translation and are inadmissible. Like burying a capsule in the backyard, putting some trace of yourself on some little pages for the eyes of some intimate eavesdropper you'll never meet is an act of something like faith, akin to those old poems whose sole purpose was to seduce some woman you hardly knew but imagined could hold your hunger, at least for the length of an embrace. But she was so seldom able to contain your desperation that you just kept composing odes to every beauty you could barely see, dazzled as you were by the rays of their eyes, their Renaissance mouths and silky or wiry tresses. You should have been born in a book and settled for that, the Norton Anthology of Lost Causes, where love songs come to lay down their arms when all the losing battles have been fought.

# Roxbury Park

Roxbury Park for a baseball boy was Eden. The dusty rocky infield with its bad hops and thigh-ripping slides, the expanse of grass where you could snag fly balls to show how cool you were or knock line drives between the opposing outfield for extra bases, even the makeshift fence to separate the players from picnicking families beyond left field, combined to feel like Paradise in some early sphere of the psyche. Maybe it was the girls who sometimes came that inspired desire for heroic plays, acts of physical grace that might someday seduce those muses, their budding beauty only beginning but already irresistible, so that even now the smell of outfield grass makes you think of sex. But from third base or the batter's box you didn't know from Eros even as you embodied it, and so each throw or pitch was everything, all you needed to know and do, creating eternal presence. It put you in mind of time, anticipating, in hours before the game, whether you'd win or lose, and that was so strange, how nobody knew beforehand but only after, when the score would be plain as the story in the *Citizen*. The box score would show the world how you were hitting, and Susie Berk would write the tale of who did what, and how. Do those clips still exist? Do you, or have your cells all been replaced over all these decades, and what you are as you write of this is new, and like the moment when you dig in at the plate or take the field as if it belongs to you, your training will kick in, turning clichés into double plays with quick wrists and nimble feet around second base, or knowing exactly where the ball is going and being there when it lands in your soft glove. Before caresses, baseball was my love, and Roxbury Park was the site of that primal embrace, and through the traffic of Olympic Boulevard there is even now some trace of my voice to be heard in the shouts of boys.

# Tor House, Carmel

These rocks must have been heavy and hard as hell to haul up from the beach, and the surf now must be as gnarly as ever, gnashing the shoreline with its dark white teeth, and your hands still seem to hold on here though your ashes are buried in the garden, now tended to polite perfection for the tourists who come as pilgrims did in the twenties to catch a glimpse of your face and your stone fortress. You were a shy soul, wounded by something so grave you withdrew to observe the world's end from your front-row bluff and this cluster of granite structures where you served your muse until she left this world, and then you drank, brooded and drank and brooded and wrote some more, protected by your kids and their kids from the world that kept on ending, and is ending still—I can read it in the ocean's regular explosions and in the well-kept yards of your neighbors living on land you sold off because you needed the cash and now the taxes are even more steep and that house to the south corrupts your view of Point Lobos. I'm feeling a bit moody in these gloomy rooms with their little windows and thick rock walls and low ceilings and everything kept just so to hold your ghosts, your photos everywhere, furniture preserved, same books on the shelves now held behind wire cages so bibliophilic visitors' fingers don't get any ideas and none of your demons get loose from between the bindings. I can't believe it took me so long to find my way to this place, but I never could quite get used to the notion of following in all those fancy footsteps—Martha Graham, Charlie Chaplin, Dorothy Parker, Edna Millay, Aldous Huxley, Carl Sandburg (*The People, Yes!* of all people) and the rest who came in search of you so long since. Yet here I am with a volunteer who knows more about you than you'd want her to and is spilling what you would never have said to me. This is the way your world keeps ending, Jeffers.

# Early Girls

Or must we call them early women, as in the eighties when "girl" was a dirty word. True, there is something sweetly sexy about these nubile beauties, their firm shapes aflame with flavor at the end of summer, leading inevitably to a certain lascivious salivation at first sight of their abundance in the farmers market, and further wholesome perversions at home in the kitchen where you slice them open with a sharp knife, salt them lightly and let the juice drip down your chin even before you start to make the salad. Raw pleasures such as these are irresistible and so feel vaguely illegal, dangerous, offering strange temptations to believe in benevolence, as if life could afford to lavish these kinds of gifts indiscriminately rather than spread good fortune with such selective blessings. Early girls taste even that much sweeter at the dawn of autumn, this time when the sun's warmth is felt for what feels like the last time and the cool nights naturally foreshadow the coming cold. The quickening days can be tasted in the generous flesh of these fruits, giving themselves to our mouths as if we deserved every explosion of their finite delight. Their reds blend with my blues to make for purple prose, so sue me, at this stage of the year whoever dares to indulge themselves can plead necessity—your honor, I just can't help spilling or speaking in over-the-top tongues while possessed by these mysterious spirits, these perfect orbs of earthy delicacy which pretend to be mere food. Babes and dudes of the jury, you know they are more than that, and that we are all but innocent as we surrender to our desires. That's why these last days before fall, when travelers and students return to work and the down-on-their-luck are looking for a break to help them withstand the coming storms, you must be grateful for tomatoes and sing their praises and never take for granted their repeat appearance, their delicious presence, their bright sweetenings of September evenings when you and your friends sit down to share their favors.

# Unchained Buddha

Somebody, maybe a chipmunk, shat on the Buddha. So soon since I took the chain and Master lock from around his neck and set him on the retaining wall above the succulents. Surely it must mean good luck. But the fire truck pulling up next door at dusk and now idling in the street while the paramedics work inside does not bode well for this otherwise excellent Sunday when the swells were coming in sets for the surfing contest and the multitudes came to the cliffs for January's angle on light and dogs on leashes met up and got briefly acquainted. Like us, only more honestly animalistic, sniffing each other intimately. The fumes of the fabric softener spewing from the clothesdryer next door right through the honeysuckle are as sickening as cigarette smoke but like the skateboarders across the street and the geezers on their front porches and the squirrels tightroping along the power cables, they're part of the neighborhood ecosystem. We are all in the soup together, as Michael McClure once said, if not exactly on the same page or even in the same ballpark. We share only the street where the screeching tires and the screaming farting motorbikes compete with more indigenous noises like the rooster a few doors down, those skateboards scraping the asphalt, garage bands practicing, and of course the mockers. Why do birds sing? Why can't a man retire to his bungalow and be left alone to do nothing, instead of be driven to register every tremor on his seismograph? How much music can we take pumped through these earbuds until nothing is all we hear? The sky turns a cooler blue as soon as the sun goes under giving the evening a good shot of Beauty that outlives the flu and almost every news flash, a nuanced indigo of relief and sweet melancholy without regret, of blue gratitude for everything, every ordeal endured, every kiss. Whatever is said here stays here, as if a shrink were listening, or a confidante in bed in some Hollywood hotel. Why did the chipmunk shit on the Buddha? To be enlightened.

# Midnight in Santa Cruz

Coming out of the Art Deco darkness of the Del Mar after the late show I note it is past midnight and Pacific Avenue looks oddly twisted, the street wiggled down to one lane curling snakelike among dense foliage like the old Garden Mall and, amazingly, it is. There's no place open and I'd like a beer so I stroll over to Front Street to see who's playing at the Catalyst. It must be 1973 or so because Oganookie is into its last set and the dancers crammed in front of the bandstand have worked up a sweat and the cowboys and bikers and hippies and grad students are stomping their boots on the boards of the old carriage-house floor. The music is some kind of Boulder Creek bluegrass, blue as the smoke of cannabis leaves grown and burned in these hills, fiddle-guitar-mandolin-bass-and-banjo burning as if the musicians' fingers are aflame, possessed of some ancient backwoods juju that rocks the big room with primal rhythms that move everyone, even the bouncers and bartenders who rule the place with the force of their studly cool, and the busgirls collecting the dregs of the downed pints. This is old Santa Cruz, what's going on, have I fallen into a time warp where stoned golden ages are hallucinated, or is the past not past, as Faulkner said, or all ages contemporaneous, per that blowhard Pound? Poets are everywhere, as they were then, reading at Zachary's every chance they get or printing broadsides in Westside garages or running off their latest works on Xerox machines and scattering them about town, shamelessly promoting Romance. This was before tiny devices made hooking up so casually electronic, when you had to seduce your sex object by serenading her until she swooned into your arms against her sisters' advice. Those were the days, or so they seem from this distance, under the influence of senior discounts, reimagining your twenties in some surf-crashed redwooded Left Bank or Montparnasse of the mind. The time is real, is now; it is you who have passed.

# Facing West from California's Shores

STEEP SLOPE, STAY BACK, DANGER, says the sign, and a small dog is barking between the beats of a pop song pumped from the speakers of an SUV while its driver surveys the surf through binoculars. Parked in a row at the state park, in the 20-minute lot overlooking Natural Bridges beach, we note the pearl-gray glow of the ocean glazed by the sinking sun through cirrus clouds above the horizon. There's a boat out there to focus the eye and calm the Pacific, normally not too peaceful but seemingly sleepy now; it humanizes the water by ripping fish by force from its layered dark. Gazers lean on the fence in an oxygen-induced daze, and a young mom stares into her phone while her boy bounces about in the front seat of their compact sedan. Sea gulls shmooze, pelicans hang loose on craggy rocks. So this is social life, being alone with others in our cars, or out of doors, or across a table at lunch with a glass of wine. Across the arroyo the mobile homes have come to look almost as comfortable as the cormorants on the last stone arch still standing. Iceplant grips the cliff to hold the coast in place lest a tourist slip and somebody gets sued. One's step must be closely watched here. How will these views go on forever otherwise? Attention needs to be paid. Devices with screens have less to reveal than the quiet clouds with no reception whatever. You keep returning to the same crime scene, retracing your steps to find the trail of wrong turns that brought you here to muse on the lucky breaks that saved your life. They still hurt, they don't heal, and yet some greater violation has been avoided, some fatal injury evaded by way of accidental serendipity, blind chance, random paths crossing just in time to rescue the errant pilgrim from his own passionate attachment to what could have killed him otherwise. This is why he sits stupefied watching the sun go down and wondering. Breathing the blue-green air and giving thanks.

# *Terroirisme,* or Proust at the Wine Bar

The taste of this Soquel red whose name is Noir speaks a language of lost time on my tongue listening to old songs and finding echoes of Old San Jose Road years ago where I met bobcats or coyotes prowling from time to time, heard owls some nights, or loud bees swarming as they moved their hive, and wild girls rode their bikes five miles uphill to find me at home with just such sips of blood-deep crimson to sweeten and darken some warm afternoons. That road still curls past schools and farms and Seventh Day Adventist conference grounds and Subud House where Sufi square dances or something comparably occult occurred, redtail hawks cutting long curves through cool blue sky harassed by redwing blackbirds protecting their turf. You could pull over and buy fresh eggs if you knew where to turn, or hike up the creek and meet babes on horseback who asked you to speak to their mounts to keep them from spooking. The flavor of those days has a long finish, a strong bouquet of bay and redwood duff and poison oak and thorny blackberry bushes that pierced your flesh as you picked their sweet, dark, fingertip-staining fruit. The oaks and madrones that escaped the stove spoke of deer and fox scat on the forest floor, strangely rhyming with the scat of jazz singers so urbane their voices ring almost as clear as cricket choruses keeping the beat in the quiet of a summer night. *For all we know, we may never meet again,* they seem to sing, though maybe what they are saying is *This is eternity, this is eternity, this is eternity,* repeating these rhythmic riffs like happy frogs croaking and thirsty creeks rippling as if forever after the gift of a wet winter. The trees are multi-instrumentalists whose reeds are played by sensuously shifty winds or subtle breezes that stroke your face like familiar fingers. Just listen to this local wine and taste its earthy whispers moistening your lips with something like kisses.

# Mission Street

The original mission was to convert the locals, and this road ran down to the plaza where the church was built and the white-collar workers leaned on the heathens in hopes of saving their souls. Now it is also known as Highway One and its couple of commercial miles are lined with offices and shops and taquerías and fast-food franchises, pharmacies and strip malls and a monstrous Safeway, nail salons, liquor stores, surf shops and Laundromats, a medical clinic, a psychic, schools and pizza places. Pedestrians take their chances even in the crosswalks marked by blinking lights, and bicyclists take their lives on wheels and sometimes lose them and are temporarily commemorated with a few bouquets, and drivers at certain times of day or on those weekends when the tourists are running must have patience with the traffic jams, which keep them backed up past the gas stations listening to talk shows or personal music programmed into their heads to muffle the sirens screaming past toward some accident or dope smugglers or poachers up the coast. And even through the haze of carbon particles spewed from tailpipes the ocean can be smelled in the steady breeze and the smell of fried food whips past in the wake of a passing truck whose diesel fumes are Proustian in their evocation of foreign cities where that smell was everywhere and you were young and even sewage spelled adventure by association. Now you cross that street or drive it nearly every day, it is the artery in or out of town, the address of restaurants to which you like to walk, the location of that café or tasting room where you pick up a loaf of bread sometimes or sip some wine because they are close to home. But even on days you don't, you're glad they are there because they civilize the neighborhood. The power lines are buried so the birds have no place to hang, and the trees are small, and the pedestrians few and mostly homeless, and your mission is to record what you can as the cars roll past.

# Barrio Santa Cruz

The whitewashed walls, the cobblestones, the gift shops with mementos of Seville, Buñuel's blinding camera angles catching the stylized light, and so close to the Alcázar and to the river and the Gypsies on the other side, this labyrinth of little streets and plazas, and little patios and courtyards enclosing quiet privacies, the old magnolias erupting unexpectedly, the oranges, lemons, dark eyes, olive skin, all the flamenco romance of an exile's memory-drenched poems engulf you as you stroll, as if there were nothing more important to do than immerse yourself in his melancholy the better to see through his eyes and smell through his nose and feel through his sun-browned skin the heat and warmth of these historic streets, taking a few steps in the lost footprints and having the same transience. These days near the Guadalquivir are rare and you must be aware of everything you are losing, all those Spanish glances and the long counters heaped with savory dishes in the bars and the tilework trimming the white plaster and the heavy wooden doors with iron hardware and the terra cotta roofs, your own strangeness somehow at home, like his, the poet who never returned except in words. That's why you have to be him, keeping alive awareness of a hometown that was his and that nourished his earliest sensory understanding of chance's erotic generosity, its random gifts in the way of native neighborhoods whose childhood grasp of the magical persists. It seems right here though it was long ago you first set foot there during a drought and the guitars you heard were either yours because they were just under your balcony, or his because he caught them on paper and sent them back from afar, you can hardly tell because time by now has had its way with you and turned you inside out so much you'll never find your way back to who you were or where you read it. The arch through which you walk is the one whose curve returns to cover your tracks so that even later no one will know you were here.

# Little Dume

I saw your electrifying Bride of Frankenstein hair as you cruised by in your Volkswagen bus going the other way on the Coast Highway and wondered who in the world such a woman could be, so when I walked into your bookstore and saw you, well, what could I do but ask you to dinner sometime and seduce you and spend the next few months on the bluff with you in our love nest, two young beautiful birds without a clue but coming alive to the big smoggy bay with its circle of lights at night and smashing waves and more stars than over all of LA. It was just a few steps down rotting stairs to the beach where the surf was perfect and I was the only Jewish dude in sight among all the blonds—with books, no less, on the shelves of our one-room shack with its flagstone fireplace—and the surfers didn't know what to make of me as I swam waves the next break over. Were we golden or what, even though I was just coming back from the underworld where I had madness to burn and met such strangeness as I am still discovering and trying to put together in words like some origami puzzle, but much tougher, so our moment with our incompatible cats and funny conversations and fantastic orgasms was just what sanity—or at least my psyche—demanded, the way serendipitous turns of fortune reliably arrive, or big surf delivers you in a rush you just need to ride. Above that gully I gathered my wits, and you brought the soul back into my grateful body. Those windows on the curved coastline rhymed with reflections in your eyes and your tight curls, and we rode those waves right into our lives. That cove has changed but it is in us, I can still see the changes in the gray sky, and hear the way the wind off the ocean arouses the trees, and smell the iceplant and the pines and the eucalyptus smoke on the little patio looking out at everything.

# Shades of Lady Day

My hand is stamped, the sold-out show has adjourned for intermission and I am admitted to replace someone who needs to get up for work tomorrow and has freed a seat. Lady Day is in town, or her facsimile who channels or translates from the existing record of the original. I have walked for an hour downtown, sent a fax at FedEx, passed by every bar and bistro I wasn't hungry or thirsty enough to sit in and listen and steal what might be eavesdropped from the clientele, browsed among my recurrent used music and books in Logos and returned with luck to await the second set. I know I'm getting old when I'm happy to see cops cruising lower Pacific to keep the gang-bangers from killing each other and casual passersby, and the bums and buskers from bothering shoppers looking for holiday bargains, discounts begging customers to come in the door and spend some rent money while there's time. It's getting warm, I remove my scarf and jacket, blue beret stuffed in the left pocket (berets are cool because they keep your head warm and can be easily stashed), look from this corner over the humming room where the capacity crowd now on their feet seem happy, imagine that, to stand and gab at ease with friends some Monday night in eternity and, when the lights blink, find their seats to escape deeper into the music. In the dark club Billie's story is spelled out none too subtly between numbers by the singer, and her sound is close enough to give the seniors something to remember, or imagine anyway, trying to hear what is beyond recovery, a smoke-like echo in a smoke-free zone where no ghost is safe from those who would bring it back from oblivion for the price of a night out. Who wouldn't be nostalgic for that sublimely suffering, unreachable, irreplaceable sound, a wispy trace of some lost notes immortally sad in their absence, where silence is unacceptable because it sends us back to ourselves.

# Post Office

Slow down. Take time, as you stand in line, to smell the roses on the FOREVER stamps, or to admire the handsome form of that body doing business at the counter, or to marvel at the overlooked murals overhead, or to imagine the look on the face of the friend who will open your package in a few days and be delightfully surprised. Your wait here is a chance to meditate, to support the service you still need despite all the virtual alternatives: the actual transport and delivery of words on paper. The person sneezing behind you just has allergies, nothing catching, and think of the places the people in the passport line are headed once their mug shots are affixed to their documents— one of the old countries where relatives still live and will be thrilled to see them, or some tropical shore where the water is warm and the smoothies spun from indigenous fruits and juices. You can read the front page of *The New York Times,* if you had the two bucks plus tax, and learn that the world is still violently corrupt, and the hot politicians still horny, and the basketball players still bargaining for more millions. Which reminds you, you need some commemorative stamps with immortal athletes on them, and some flat-rate priority mailers, and maybe a few of those scenic landscapes an inch across to remind you what your letters will be flying over. The post office is a sacred space of human communication, boxholders coming and going with their handfuls of fresh mail, maybe a love letter in there somewhere; old friends gossiping briefly, surprised to meet; a face you've seen from time to time but never met over many years, aged but recognized. Now you are next up. You consider whether to send the book via media mail and save a few cents or splurge for first class and expedite its arrival. "May I help the next person in line?" says the clerk—he's talking to you, polite as the Highway Patrol, or the airline pilot giving your words wings.

# Inside *The Sun*

From my corner desk upstairs behind the banks of blue glass at Union and Cedar, I felt I could see almost everything in the city, the whole population passing by below at some point in the workday, which we chronicled weekly in our slim pages of print. That great black walnut across the street cast its green shade over the parking lot behind the bakery and the coffee roasters and the other café in the courtyard behind the bookshop, all those brick walls doomed to fall in the earthquake. Foot traffic there was magical in the mundane way of unexpected sightings of miscellaneous citizens—one's ex-loves or former landlords, strangers engaged in intense dialogue among the parked cars, troubled bicyclists muttering to themselves some homeless lament or belting out pained arias in the intersection. Inside our office the ad sales reps were filing their copy and the art department were bent over their drawing boards, X-acto knives in hand, cutting their designs precisely for pasteup, while the editors hammered their keyboards to the beat of the reggae tapes in the production room where Rose at the monstrous machine set every word of the newspaper in type. Crossing the street on the way to lunch you might meet, stopped at the corner, someone who leaned out their car window and yelled encouragement or criticism, like a letter to the editor, acknowledging your role as a medium for what mattered in their world. Back at the desk with your deli sandwich on deadline, you made a few calls to check facts, banged out the last lines of your column or edited the story that came in late and penned a headline across the top. There was harmonious timing in that steady pace of collective improvisation creating the new issue, while outside the town went on with its odd routine of extemporaneous drama—a couple kissing in public, a merchant pensively shuffling down the sidewalk, a boy with a skateboard waiting for the bus, a girl with a dancer's stride—oblivious of your effort to catch the time.

# Near Broadway and Columbus

In search of the perfect notebook I am cruising Chinatown. The discount gift and kitsch store shelves are brimming with useless crap of every kind to seduce the tourists shopping for souvenirs amid the smells of herbs and ginseng, fish and dim sum, greens and green tea up and down the street where on a weekday afternoon in splendid weather camera-carrying families swarm in several languages. Upstairs in City Lights the silent poets wait it out in the afterlife, their volumes patiently through thin and thinner poised like shelter cats to be selected by customers desperate for company. Outside, the avenue slopes downhill and uphill as on any other Heraclitean day, fires cooking in a thousand kitchens, pizzas baking, garlic simmering, espressos being brewed in cafés where ladies eat ice cream and gossip happily in their widowhood. Bums and yuppies savor the sun of Washington Square Park and the spires of St. Peter and Paul's seem to gleam with all but divine light. At Capp's and O'Reilly's baseball games are being played on TVs above the bar, and yet how close around these corners ghosts of drunken beatniks haunt the alleys with their mournful tales of spiraling decline. Ferlinghetti would have none of it, refusing to stagger into that dark vortex, climbing instead the stairs of his business up to his office on the second floor to gaze out over the neighborhood with the stamina of a survivor and all the crafty gratitude of one who invented luck. And how did such good fortune befall me even to live this long and to witness the endless spectacle of these streets, these shops, these eateries, some of which I know well enough to walk in as if I belong there and make my way directly to the men's room. Where are the strippers of yesteryear? Replaced by nimbler babes and newer barkers touting their charms to passing pedestrians. Even without caffeine I am wide awake, trying to find my place in the proceedings, Year-of-the-Dragon pen speaking in tongues of black ink on compact pages bound in boards of nearly Chinese red.

# Old Standards

The singer's tea is steeping on a stool beside the piano, leaving a warm ring on the set list it shares the round seat with, and the trio is warming up the full house with a standard until the vocalist takes the stage in her pixilated black frock and impeccable technique routinely reiterated in club after club for so many years she can run these riffs in her sleep à la Ella, who could outscat any six castrati at the Supreme Court arguing the case for sweet-voiced sentiment in the face of the unspeakable. One must dress in black like the sidemen because of the grief, and one must sing with the logic of a mockingbird mimicking whoever you last heard lamenting their hard luck in the lost language of some subtropical port where even the stevedores lift their burdens in bossa nova and after the last shift sip *caipirinhas* in the harbor bars and talk about missing señoritas in bikinis from beaches beyond resurrection because the sand has long since slipped through the waist of the hourglass. There is always time to kiss time goodbye the longer you last to warble your chaste heartbreak under a useless moon in early spring when the cruelest music pours from old speakers in rooms where records ran circles around your blues because you heard them spinning in your muse's arms. Such tunes recur forever because the years are circular, always returning in maturing forms to deepen what's gone in a way that feels unending like the seasons themselves in one weather, one sweet smell or another. One voice can move through many moods in the course of a concert, just as a single soul can feel almost infinitely affiliated with like-minded psyches and bodies too smitten to see what's coming, which is where the lovesick refrains come from. Hear that? It's not a heartbeat but the stand-up bass impersonating that artery in the throat you loved to run your tongue along and taste its salty sweetness on deep summer nights in the same city where the concrete seems to soften only under the influence of certain melancholy melodies.

# Rites of Night

These rites may seem obscure to some, but they satisfy a primal desire to praise a presence that isn't there, some wiry or willowy spirit whose breath still blows through visiting brass or just some intimate instrument which leaves a trail of quiet hieroglyphs to be deciphered later by librarians or obscure scholars researching what couldn't have been said otherwise in dusty stacks where they may meet, as in some cheap romance, a comparably compromised eccentric in search of the same surprise, a rhythm they can concur on, and they kiss, and next thing they embrace in a perverse bond entwined with certain texts and sex unlike anything they've read. Music is read too by those so attuned, and heard when the sound insinuates itself like an idea of timeless delight, a state of suspended ease when the soul is taken to another place on the strength of song's wings. How many ways are there to say the same thing, a surge of words that can't be explained and don't quite spell themselves out but hold fast to enchantment in hopes of transcendence, a primitive drive to register and soar. Thrift-shop psychoanalysis will never reduce the sauce of the unconscious to something you could spread on your Burnt Norton and consume like French toast in lieu of the infinite kiss that keeps on though it has long since moved on to other mouths and now speaks its sweet genius into ears no longer yours. And this is why you must take her music into your hands and turn it to your ends, run with it until it wears you out, make it yours in a way no one else will, recollect whatever you can with or without tranquility and put those powerful feelings in their place before they overflow. It is a turquoise night and the sky holds the light of lengthening day and the rain has taken a break, and this is just a way of measuring time as it streams through the stylus of the instrument, drawing a sad sound from the turning disc, spinning timelessness from this.

# Neighborhood Watch

Some afternoons, after lunch, in summery weather when the sun is above the house leaving the front deck in the shade and blue light is radiating off the bay and Monterey is a purple profile sloping toward the Pacific in the distance, I like to sit outside with a smoke or a cool drink and ogle the neighborhood. It's often quiet except for the song of a mockingbird, or the obnoxious scream of a leafblower down the street, or a sneaky Prius whose wheels on the asphalt are its only sound, or trios of teenagers yakking as they stroll past unaware of their incidental eavesdropper, or the occasional solo squawker on a cellphone obliviously disturbing the peace. Dog walkers with their plastic shit-collecting sacks, sleek *biciclistas* whizzing by, couples of various ages getting their exercise, free-range cats, motorcycle riders, kids on skateboards make this street like any other in a smallish town where people can sometimes see and be seen outside the shells of their cars. Way down the coast the smokestacks of the power plant pump their white puffs cloudlike into the sky. Doing nothing is a fine art learned from long hours of looking, listening, sniffing the smell of Brussels sprouts breezing in from up the coast, associating that smell with previous seasons whose seductive allure is bound with the pull of youth on increasingly seasoned recollection that can't quite hold what it lost, cannot collect what it recalls. When the cops pay a call on the kids next door, I'm merely curious, no longer worried about my own suspicious activities, a sure sign of maturity. Abandoned shopping carts left on Mission Street, just a few blocks away, speak a language of other lost things. Sirens of the Highway Patrol are swearing out loud that accidents happen, and the exhaust of buses and trucks is settling subtly on every exposed surface. Who else would pause to observe such atmospheric disturbances but a pure voyeur, a self-taught street-watcher, a freelance vigilante, a neighbor with nothing better to do than keep an eye out for whatever might rise to amaze.

# Live Music at Moe's Alley

Who put the red dye in the Maraschino cherry? What lip gloss is this on the rim of my glass? Whose face so imprinted itself on the surviving psyche the stain remains decades later? Such riddles will not be solved however syncopated or synchronized the band's heartbending noise as it drives hard into its first groove and the dancers take the floor to shake off the daze of their day jobs and the endless heartache of relentless age—each day an advance toward a soundless end where no lark nor tuba can reach with its unique speech. And how tight are your lines, o esteemed soloist, do your harmonies align with such exquisite precision that those who hear them leap to their feet, or at least are moved by their truth to fill the available space with wiggling struts of lust transformed into something more like fun? It means what it does, even the geezers can see that, moving their sneakers subtly but happily over the dark floor, which gleams with the bright force of such timely feet. If the man unfolding his roll of bills at the bar ordering two more beers is to be believed, a scent of aftershave or talc is meant to veil the truth of sweat. What is the real aroma of such a night—a synthesis of women's skin you've known over so many years you can't even count? The smoke floating in from outside where insomniacs take their medicine in the street or in the parking lot of Toys R Us and the shut-forever doors of Circuit City? Or is it merely the odor of soap from the men's room where even now the revelers pause to urinate, as I did just before the break. Who still takes their songs on the road in hopes some lonesome babe will praise their sound and embrace its bluest truths? And as for you, you will finish your second pint, catch as much of the second set as you can stand, then climb into your car and retire across town, where your silent wifeless bed awaits and the morning promises coffee and solitude.

# Summer Travelers

On the coast road, where crews are fixing the bridges and perpetually patching the pavement, there are one-lane stretches where pilot cars lead one-way traffic north and south, the summer travelers idling with their motors running en route to the next little town or inn whose economy depends on their dollars, the dinners bought, festivals attended, souvenirs picked up in the gift shops, crafty handmade artifacts, even the scenic photographs clicked from a car window—all keep the countryside humming with commerce that keeps the innkeepers in business and the locals employed. Along the rivers and inland creeks the wineries are alive, vineyards climbing the hills in rigorous rows and the tasting rooms full of sippers and designated drivers who imbibe anyway, summer is only for now and these are the pleasures of the getaway, tomorrow we may die so one must get drunk, as Baudelaire demanded, and find in the hot valleys sensations absent back where work awaits. Joy is your job this time of year in the window between then and whenever, and the days take on a transience heightened and held still by the sun, whose light is made more mild by these cool drinks and savory views and plates of local food. We are in California and even the antiques are like new with a patina of time that refreshes in its memory, its historic evidence rubbed deep by hands that touch nothing now but whose unseen traces give value to objects otherwise taken for junk. Nothing is wasted on you, even the miles that led here, to the roadside emporium, the pottery studio, the café on the plaza where a pretty waitress brings your Arnold Palmer with a smile summery in its warmth, and a sharp reminder of smiles gone by. What will we find to hold in the tired mind growing more autumnal by the hour, fog banks closing in on the cliffs and darkness seeping up from the ocean floor at dusk—only the fleeting sweetness of long afternoons that led to a bed somewhere and a leisurely embrace with your love in a rented room.

# Riverside Drive

Boomboxes blasting in the street downstairs, car alarms going off, the summer sunset driving us outside to escape the heat, but then those fights, and the view of New Jersey across the river, the silver trees of winter with their naked arms like ours, your face in subtle window light so late at night we felt we had the city to ourselves, and we did, it was ours by possession, possessed as we were, becoming so much ourselves we were almost the same person and so we exploded, pieces flying apart and landing everywhere, and I guess that's just as well because now I can sit on the front deck with only the sound of a rooster proud of himself half a block down and some NPR talk show echoing from a parked car across the street and think about Riverside Drive where we lived those years so long ago we can hardly know what occurred, it's a blur in time that's left a smear on our souls, Karen the crackhead on Broadway rapping wackily at passersby, Jerusalem Felafel with its sublime baba ganoush, the M5 with those profiles like portraits in the lighted windows as we boarded the bus to become art, rolling through the city watching the show and being it at the same time, our drama as tragic as the next passengers' but more fun because we were loved, and when we came home if we didn't kill each other we would be stirring a sauce and boiling pasta or reading delicious books or having the transcendental sex that got us into this mess, that stayed in our skin as it drove us into exile, so that even from this far I can see the leaves getting thick bright green on the park's trees as spring turns and the barges on the river haul their garbage out to sea and the factories on the far shore gleam calmly on a sunny Saturday and some other lovers live their own legend in our old apartment, maybe it's us in some parallel world where time is a wild loop and we are its willing spools.

# Younglove Avenue

It's only three blocks long, between Mission Street and the circle with the church, hardly an avenue really, but the train tracks slashing through it at an angle give it a greater scope because as you ride across them carefully on your bike so as not to slip you can look both ways and imagine long trips in a boxcar. So maybe the street is bigger than it seems, and when you lived there for a year it certainly was, opening both ways (not to speak of the journeys along those rails) toward unpredictable loves, the ones you knew and the ones you pursued and those who showed up at your door at midnight just to amaze you. The fire station across the street was where you voted, and the kid next door who mowed your meager lawn was paid with your little portable TV because you needed some excuse to give it away, you had no use for the televised lives of stars because your own was already almost too romantic to take, so many ballads going at once you needed a few more bodies to play them all, more guitars, more typewriters, more ballpoint pens, more songs. Fast forward a couple of decades to another house a block or so down on the other side of the street, where in a rented room behind the kitchen you took little naps on break on production night when your newspaper was about to be put to bed. Your paramour's spare bike was kept with hers in back and after work some summer evenings you'd take them out through the neighborhood whose cooking smelled eternal both for what it suggested about your dinner and for its aromatic echoes, neither here nor there yet all-pervasive, more total recall than you can bear. Younglove Avenue, who gave it that name, as if knowing it would set the stage for such passions, and that so many more years would pass before you'd know how long you could hold what happened there in your heart, something you'll never understand and are still in search of.

# Office Hours

Look for me anywhere whenever, as in those cracks where hours slip and time pauses for a few beats and we can talk. We'll have to improvise an assignment, like a performance piece where you sit onstage at a café table sipping a fizzwater and composing an ode to the audience, which is mesmerized by their smartphones and doesn't even notice you're up there. This frees you to be yourself, as if you had a choice, and confess you have no entertainment to offer, only the same old confessions, and that's why you've come to see me, to consult about your violations and which ones are most marketable, or whether they're just too raw, not scandalous enough, half-baked, coitus interruptus, not really satisfying and definitely not redemptive, there's nothing to save. Instead you want to reveal your innermost normality, your absolute averageness, and nevertheless your exceptional strangeness because even you can't believe your eyes, the most mundane phenomena opening infinitely in a blink, those pedestrians for example not even staggering under their history though each of them must be at least as melodramatic as yours. That's why we can meet anyplace and converse indefinitely, we have no deadline but death itself and so it's urgent we settle everything right away, like who is the student and who the teacher and who pays for the drinks. Better leave the door open lest we harass each other, and if anyone asks, it never happened. I lost my position ages ago because of something like this, remember? You were my instructor and that was illegal because you were underage so when our roles reversed the administration couldn't make heads or tails of our transgressions. I was suspended, expelled, exiled and licensed to give only the most intimate seminars where no more than one scholar at a time would be corrupted by my revelations. You got away without my recommendation—though I could have told them everything—and that's why I posted these office hours, so you might come back and we could discuss what went wrong and how it turned out this way.

# Coyoacán

With my round shades and long hair I must have looked Lennonesque because when a school bus came by kids leaned out its windows yelling "John Lennon!" I didn't get the chance to disabuse them because the bus kept going, passing the pastel walls with broken glass along the top, walls that enclosed quiet patios where private lives took place among painted tiles and others baked to a deep pink and arches and timbers and maybe a little fountain, where Trotsky and Cernuda and various other exiles had landed but also locals like Frida and Diego before they were discovered and turned into mass-market icons. Their house, which was really hers, was all but deserted except for a guard or two because now it was a sleepy museum where every now and then a couple like us, one native, one curious gringo, would show up and take over the place, mixing our myth with theirs, the former residents, or embellishing it with our own accidents, meeting at the museum where I was mesmerized at first sight by your face, so when you walked up and spoke to me I thought this must be a dream, and I was doomed for three years by your beauty the likes of which I'd never seen before, and by your quick tongue full of Marxist repartee, Palestinian passion and Mexican kisses. That's why I flew down there in aircraft that bumped over the mountains and bounced on landing opening the overhead bins, and why you flew up here after the earthquake to raise money and make posters and sleep with that artist, and why I was in Coyoacán with you that afternoon, when we walked through Frida's house and studio and looked at the remains of a romance even more epic and heartbroken than ours, more full of cruelty, we just couldn't figure out how to transplant ourselves either way, and so we were able to mate only halfway, without a bridge between our habitats to keep us comfortably apart. But you showed me your city in all its chaos, and that calm neighborhood of the painted walls.

# Car Wash

The glass-patchers make their hard pitch for fixing the nicks in your windshield so it won't shatter or craze into spiderweb cracks while you're tooling up the 280 to Cupertino. It seems like just last week when you were having the grime and dust and crushed insects of the 101 washed off, and now you are back because the steady drizzle of fallout from the exhaust pipes of Mission Street has been topped off by a fly-by bird accurately crapping on your window and so you are performing the Stations of Sisyphus in their most mundane manifestation—like doing laundry or washing dishes or shopping for groceries, which is your next stop, the quotidian tasks of a Thursday afternoon when the spouse has returned from the dry cleaner with those gossamer plastic bags and the shared car. The air machine is blowing the water off each vehicle as it rolls out of the chute and the guys in blue shirts and baseball caps are finishing them off with small towels and spray bottles of blue-tinged cleaner fluid and the metal and paint are gleaming in the hard sun of rush hour at the edge of summer. Quality Parts & Service, says the wall across the street with an arrow pointing more or less at me. I am not paranoid and yet I take everything personally lately including the postal clerk's routine courtesy as he hands me my change for a package of printed matter I've just sent into posterity via media mail. I am a medium, with any luck, and male last time I looked, and my parts are still serviceable as far as they go but who knows how much longer until the ink runs out. These instruments of mobility must be clean and capable of taking one deeper into the everyday where everything happens and passes into eternity only if noticed as if for the first time, like the glint off the sunglasses of the young mom climbing with her kid into their Honda. Waving his damp rag, the detail man delivers the keys enabling me to proceed into the sunset.

# Davenport Roadhouse

The night is young, yet old by local time, sun barely down beyond the abandoned cement plant and the sky streaked with cerise and the white trail of a fighter jet like a line of coke over the ocean. The bartender mixes me a Bonny Doon gimlet before she goes home for the night, and instead of Ugly Beauty as advertised—a rotating combo of cool jazzmen—a Spanish guitarist is strumming Andalusian riffs as I sit monklike at the bar sipping a last cocktail. Now he is fingering something that sounds like Sor, or Albéniz, one of those maestros who cries in his gazpacho lamenting whatever is lost: land, a lover, time itself having migrated leaving only these notes in the late August air. The night's final diners are finishing their dinners and a smoky aroma drifts from the kitchen as I nurse my watery drink, a cool-off lap after a hot day with such sorrows and pleasures as can only be recorded in writing lest they vanish with everything else, the morning's tomatoes and fresh cut flowers at the farmers market, the hard-luck laments of friends, the daily pages of bad news consumed with perfectly brewed coffee, which almost compensates for all the crime and corruption ravaging the world— half the state ablaze, so-called civilization everywhere wracked with massacres, the planet in agony—by sweetening its own delicious bitterness, chiaroscuro sketches on the tongue that savors every last darkness, and then the sun warming the open windows, thick letter from the last of the paper correspondents slapping the floor by the front door, and all the drama on earth right there in the post office of his Texas town under a sky so much crueler than this one, whose blast-furnace heat can be felt in the black strokes of his hand as he reports what escapes him even as he writes. We are reduced to scribes of our own erasure, like the sound of the solo guitar moaning its transient lament without even a page to scrawl or a stamp to send it. The moon is thinning and summer is coming to an end.

# Silver Lake

After your first affair with someone else, I flew down to see you in the poet's house you were renting briefly in the early days of our breakup, seven seemingly endless years of sticky and slippery goodbyes that never quite took, never were able to extract ourselves from the silken web of our oneness, and so we kept on fighting except, as when I arrived that evening, we were tangled spirit and flesh in something greater than pleasure, and the neighborhood with its hilly streets and tropical trees and little city views through telephone wires was turned to our honeymoon suite, our paradise lost after our morning communion, where we hiked and took pictures in the ruins under the summer sun, and drove to the beach where we swam in the mild surf near the sewage outfall and let the leftover salt, which we tasted later, dry on our darkening skin before window shopping at the pedestrian mall, you in your cutoff shorts and white t-shirt draped on your long bones, me in that striped top I'd bought in some shop in New York, both of us seemingly content after such completion, such solar power, such physical perfection, and yet when we returned to Silver Lake the unmade poet's bed summoned us to savor the afternoon's last light in our mouths, and so we closed that day, relaxed and possessed, wondering how this could ever end, and yet it did, and even though decades have come and gone with lots of juice under the bridges, and a lifetime and a continent have intervened, that night sealed Eden between us, and it can't be undone even this long after, so while I bask in a Saturday afternoon from another century, our history is within, and sometimes it erupts unsolicited, and alarms go off and I must get up and throw on my gear and slip down the pole and onto the truck to fight this fire again, and if it hurts to read, imagine the gratitude it signifies, and grief, but only the kind all mythic lovers suffer, and fools who lost what they loved best.

# Loring and Wyton

It was a corner in Holmby Hills where friends of my parents lived who let me park in their driveway when I was living at home and commuting to UCLA. A few blocks east of campus in that luxy and leafy neighborhood, just the right walking distance for my meditative hikes under the trees that in springtime smelled like semen, the house was a place I never entered, nobody ever seemed home, but it made for a safe location where my days began and ended as a freshman whose intellect was just awakening and then a sophomore whose brain was catching fire under the influence of distant professors whose lectures in big halls and whose assignments were incendiary—Plato, Tolstoy, Rilke, Whitman, Chekhov, Blake, Cervantes—old white guys, teachers and writers alike, who razed my suburban boyhood to its naked vacancy only to reveal the most amazing universe I'd met in my slight years, a little twit who didn't have a clue but was hungry for everything opening on that campus—the books, which I could touch and all but possess, the beautiful girls beyond my reach, a worldly atmosphere brimming with possibility, the opening days of adulthood, dawn of something astonishing yet to come. Some teachers were even approachable and I took advantage of their office hours just to get close for a few minutes to someone living a life of the mind—I wanted to bring them home to show my folks, in those days of deadly dinners, that conversation was possible, that there was something worth discussing beyond the war, that what I was reading and thinking was so much more than academic, that minds were alive and so was I in a way I never understood before and didn't yet but lusted for. So that walking back to my car at the end of the day, under those seminal oaks of Wyton Drive, lugging my books in that clunky olive-green attaché case Grandma had given me and still too square to know how dorky I looked, poetry was taking possession of me.

# Hoover Road

Over the rickety bridge across Virginia Brook you drove uphill past the homes of the Jehovah's Witness construction foreman and his wife the Amway saleswoman, and the hippie polygamist from New Jersey, and the retired Marine captain, and beyond that the bankrupt publisher and the classical guitarist and the misanthropic hermit and his prisoner wife, and the old dairy farmer with his last cow and the Mormon family with their dream mansion, to 354—the oldest house in the valley, all redwood, going back to the Gold Rush, with floors that sloped in the corners to the wood foundation that rested right on the dirt—which was my place. The neighbor above me, dressed every day in khakis and smoking his Marlboros, sprayed tons of poison into his garden to keep the weeds down and the insects dead, and it made me wonder what made its way into my well, but once you let the iron settle the water tasted good, and in those hills six miles from the bay it was sunny most of the time when it wasn't raining. Seventeen years at home there were enough to give the illusion of living forever, looking back on the bodies of dozens of loves and lovely or pointless couplings and failures to find relief with random women who only proved my solitude more profound than they could cure, and yet so many were more than I deserved with such faces as can still be summoned in all their illusory truth, that beauty burned into memory like a brand, my personal evidence of possession, possessed as I was by passion and such passing gratifications. What meals were cooked in that kitchen with my constantly evolving collages all over the walls, what cords of fragrant wood went up in the granite fireplace that crashed in the earthquake, what pages and pages of poems and prose were typed and retyped on the Adler, on the flea-market Royal, scrawled in ruled books like this one where I tried to record what I couldn't fathom. I wanted to harvest what felt immortal for a minute as it was lost.

# A Walk on the Wharf

*Do not feed birds, No dogs, No alcohol* are three commandments spelled out on the signs, and the seals belowdecks are honking their usual song, and gangs of seagulls squawk like backup singers. Even a shy pelican is discreetly friendly, standing on a rail in the solstice light with herds of cumulus floating out to sea after a storm. It's an almost impossibly Mediterranean day in California just before the apocalypse, which is always coming right up. Like that of the birds and the clouds our transience is sweet and bitter to savor when we have a minute to think about the wave spray combing Steamer Lane with just a few surfers the size of dust specks even though up close their shoulders are wide and their sun-raked hair and skin show the weather's sculptural humanism. Despite the alcohol ban you can buy a drink in any of the bars, and the tchotchke shops have every souvenir you can think of to add to your vacation museum— that room at home where you keep the stuff that proves you were someplace once. Time is like that, slowly erasing everything but the mementos, and it's okay, you can take it, but when it starts taking your dear ones you take it personally. So it's helpful to stroll out here for an hour and hang with the birds and the eternally salty fisherman. There is something to be said for fish & chips and for the touristic taverns with views of the bay where ancients can gaze out at leisure, drinking in the slanted light. Across the parked cars you can see the distant peninsula like a reclining nude and Loma Prieta closer to the north and in the foreground a town curled up around its rollercoaster. Your eyes can hardly believe what they see, it is too beautiful and strange no matter how mundane. When the wind picks up and stings as it slices your face you want to stay on this bench as long as you can because the afternoon sun could be the last of its kind.

# Central Park

A few trees may have snapped in the storm but plenty are still standing on this splendid Monday at the end of November when just a few people are strolling along or walking their dogs or pushing their old folks in wheelchairs. A lone runner, a little girl kicking the piles of dry leaves, a guy around my age grinning in the sweet sunlight as he ambles toward 59th Street. What a respite from the city's restlessness. The cool music of gliding blades is an antidote to the screeching wheels of the subway. The mundane workings of urban legs are almost amazing in the light of so much distress, and my pedestrian observations almost a song in the oddly silent air. Every other language overheard is foreign under the cosmopolitan sky, even my own tongue almost incomprehensible because all but speechless in the face of the inexpressible. Language is so inadequate to trace even the outlines of this existence, the baby's eyes pushed along in a stroller as puzzled as mine at the everyday display that just a few hours ago in those faces on the train felt so cruel and moody, so irritable, inconvenienced by everything. Even the ambulance siren clearing some intersection scarcely disturbs the pastoral calm in these greenish reaches of the city's heart. And always the babes in their tough boots headed somewhere only half-aware of their transient beauty as they gab with their pals en route to some romance they can scarcely imagine. Where does it end, if ever—in the demolished houses of the Rockaways? Even they can't quite eradicate what drives the bereft to try to stay alive. I wonder what happens next, we wonder, hoping to be relieved of what defeats us. What are you writing? a man asks, and I don't know what to answer. Nothing more than the quack of a passing duck, or the obligatory warbling of other birds if there were any, or the squawking radios of the Parks guys on their little electric carts making their rounds.

# Pensión Las Once

On calle Echegaray, in the heart of Madrid, the tiny lodgings, run by the Rey family—Jesús and Pepita and young Antonia, and Fernandito the garrulous parrot—were up three flights of wooden stairs shaped by centuries of residents and trudging travelers, and if you stayed out late enough you'd have to clap for the *sereno* to unlock the big doors on the street, and once inside you'd climb and ring the bell and Jesús, from his bed on the other side of the wall, would first confirm who you were then pull a string connected to the inside latch and let you in. On the ground floor was a bakery where they worked all night and just at dawn they'd load the little truck in the courtyard to take the rolls to be delivered and voices would fly up lightly like the songs of the skylarks crisscrossing in the rectangle overhead as daylight spread outside your inward-facing window. That portable typewriter you bought at the Rastro to work on your poems disturbed the peace of the whole building, echoing from your room off the five floors of walls above the patio, so Jesús had to ask you to stop at nine o'clock. He said he had known Hemingway during the civil war and that typing was fine with him but not at just any hour. Pepita was kind and round, and Antonia was shy behind her black eyes, and their cooking smelled good in the hallway, where the toilet was. You returned four times in seventeen years because it felt like home and your hosts were always there, Jesús going blind and Pepita plumper and Antonia slowly aging over a lifetime of mopping floors and making beds, and the bird calling out *"Antonia!"* as the refrain in his *repertorio,* and you the traveler glad to be back in a reliably old world, even in the days when the dictatorship had ended and modernity was dawning. Thanks to the local bars where the smoke was thick and the talk was loud you fell asleep with red wine in your veins and Spanish in your head.

# The Floating World

Usual June wind lashes the coast with cool blasts of spring, twenty years since you started haunting this house on this ridge where you came to recover from your greatest and most catastrophic romance. It took a decade and you still hadn't healed, even after moving hundreds of miles south with a new mate you ached, and now each time you return you're a ghost again tasting your own absence in this splendid landscape you can barely take anymore for its unsayable associations. You will instead contemplate historic cords of firewood stacked so rats could take up residence, garden beds dug and planted with starts of summer tomatoes, apricots picked the one year that skinny tree pumped out a multitude, Jackson the cat who came with the house and kept you company—small pleasures, good air, sounds of dancing trees. And you mustn't forget the desk where you bore down on pain to convert it into a strange energy, using your grief to produce beautiful bloodshot music, twilight purple blues of a soul turning over a new boulder, rolling it uphill as on those morning hikes to Old Stage Road to fetch the *Times*, such excellent exercise for the sick at heart. The pleasant space of the house, end-of-the-road quiet, stands of tanoaks with their knotty grace, the way the wind picks up and settles without explaining itself, throwing the sky into sharp relief, horizon blurred by haze so the coastline floats before the amazed eyes—all these things rise to ease misery when you stop and look, listen, breathe. Desolation is lifted slightly, you begin to transcend your bereaved disbelief, to overcome your own survival, to take a certain delight in the cleansing sensations, rising spirits stroking the trees into song. Was Orpheus here, or is that just an osprey crying high overhead, or ravens squawking, or some fox barking so oddly before dawn, or sea lions yakking over their loudspeakers? Twenty years and the agave have grown, perennials become better established, tables in the office achieved a Zen emptiness. And up in the loft the bed retains an aura of embraces.

# Farmers Market

Four girls perched in a row on the pickup tailgate behind the blueberries are a sight for old eyes on a Saturday morning, their dangling legs keeping time to the bluegrass band serenading the shoppers and the farmers and the faux flâneurs out for a stroll in a parking lot turned country fair for a day. The pasta man offering bargains under his baseball cap, the Happy Boys and Dirty Girls coolly flaunting their greens, the gourmet olive oil entrepreneurs with their tempting bits of bread for dipping in little golden bowls, fruit purveyors with their sweet bright hills all take me home to a farm I've never known except in old poems by aging drunks nostalgic for imagined Edens remembered precisely and harvested in language alone. The barbeque dudes are frying bacon and that primal smell almost sends you swooning, but then a whiff of tamales takes you to the force field of some taco truck where you once stopped for a quick bite with your sweetie, and from there you are taken with the fresh scent of whole-grain sourdough loaves and the bakers' freshly tanned faces. Such mornings of local travel can scarcely be matched by trips to exotic lands where other versions of the same vendors, flowers whose names escape you casting equally chromatic aromas, abundant food for the eyes seduce you the same way, only here you are close to home where you will stash your bounty for a week of savoring. And here is where you feast your nose and ears and eyes on the fullness of a week's work, or a season's, brought to fruition. These neighbors you don't know, these sky-browned faces you almost recognize, these easily circulating people who could be anyone seem to be here forever, playing their mythic roles in the mundane rituals of exchange. Chocolate, that luxury, the essential fuel of coffee, earthy potatoes, sugar-snap peas, strawberries, bunches of basil, even this cool coastal overcast tell of warm days inland when under the spell of summer you could feel your nectar sweetening in the sun.

# West Cliff Blues Again

Same wind as ever on West Cliff in the seemingly kind sun of summer's end, the star whose fire feels mild even as it fries us. Compared to the alternatives this is a good deal as ice melts everywhere and the mojitos and margaritas grow more watery while tropical storms pick up steam turning into hurricanes creaming the Gulf Coast again. From here the whitecaps look benevolent casting their wide smiles while pelican gangs flirt from a low altitude admiring their likenesses in the undulating kelp. Don't bother trying to describe this, pictures are just a hint of what was seen some perfect afternoon with nothing to say to anyone but look how much to express. The iceplant resembles green fire in front of this bench officially engraved "In Loving Memory of Jan Thompson," signed "Sharky" with a paw print, perhaps her dog, who probably walked and crapped on these paths in years gone by. Let's hope she picked it up, unlike whoever left the droppings of theirs in front of the next bench over. Everything must be accounted for because we're not Romantics anymore—it's too late even to be postmodern, so ruthlessly are we hurtled through the future. Stopping to do nothing but smell the scenery is an act of resistance against Time and the West's decline. Just note the sun's angle sliding down the sky, and the sound of those cruising motorcycles depleting the planet, not to speak of the cars, which are quieter and deadlier and which drive us. I seem to keep repeating myself, as if there were no new thing under the sun, when in truth every day there is something to be discovered. This is worth noticing at the end of August when kids are girding themselves for school and the tourists are soon to leave town and fall will come with its first kisses before things turn worse—wildfires, earthquakes, tsunamis, drought, whatever devastation awaits us. But for now those kisses are just what the philosopher ordered, those and the ones of the lips I love, a continent away yet surely returning soon.

# Failed Recluse

I've tried and failed to recuse myself from the disasters other people bring on themselves and everyone else. It seemed the wisest thing to do; the old Chinese guys did it, wrote poems about it, drank wine by the waterfall way out in the mountains where nobody but a fellow drunken poet would ever find them—but only after a life of civil service. I was too young to retire, never had a job, and every time I dropped out there were complications. In Malibu, in Soquel Valley, on Gualala Ridge I tried to be some kind of monk but there was always some fetching woman who'd prove to me that celibacy was, as Lin Yutang insisted, "a freak of civilization," or some local newspaper asking for my ink, seducing me with its promise of eyes to relish my sentences and a civic psyche to infiltrate with otherwise unspeakable thoughts. My daily rituals—the fires built, the minimalist meals, absorption of the views so that the mind was full of trees and skies and mountains and oceans endless in their embrace of everything—somehow required accompaniment despite the private satisfactions of what revealed itself so generously. Yet solitude suited me too, I knew my way around those inner sanctums, those sacred spaces where even the worst news scarcely penetrated, spaces impervious to random calamities of social life, even though simple domesticity presented its own disasters—insect plagues, plumbing ruptures, stormy blackouts to be toughed out powerless in the dark. Those nights alone in the rain, those lovely days in sunlight, also solo, were not enough to contain me, even with all those books, and so at last, half a century into a discipline begun on the bedroom floor with baseball cards or little soldiers inventing intimate miniature wars, I came down out of my aerie, out of my cave, my cabin, my cliffside cottage or ridgetop lookout, to mate for life with one of my own kind, she in her chair with a book, I at my desk. Two hermits pooling their solitude may summon the strength to negotiate the world as one.

# A Day in LA

The sun clangs off the bay with an aggressive glare, these bluffs the last refuge of a refugee returned to remember everything—from the first glimpse of these waters ages ago to this afternoon when, in a Hollywood pawn shop, he found the pearls with which to surprise his bride. And so you cruised through hard streets lined with low-rent storefronts and out-of-work residents waiting for the bus, and an hour later were driving the other way past gated lawns like moats while topless tour buses announced the fleetingly famous to a few perplexed passengers. How can one city sustain so many, he muses, unsure even which person he is, first second or third, nor whether he is singular in the way he takes it all so personally, or plural in some collective universe where everyone shares his astonishment or nostalgia or cosmic sadness over what was or wasn't. It scarcely matters at this hour in autumn, sun gradually angling into the ocean, broad beach below scribbled with tire tracks and solo strollers along the shoreline at high tide in front of the vacant lifeguard stations, the drowning out of luck on such a cool afternoon. *Cómo está la chula?* asks the dogwalker into his smartphone, and I see in the screen of mine the face of my Beautiful One, her smile eternal in the first rush of our love, and am comforted by the endurance of such a vision. I can still smell the first eucalypts, and taste the language of a Spanish poet exiled here lamenting the loss of his favorite lips now moistening someone else's a thousand miles away and half a century between. Is it a desert you are now traducing, or more like the mind's Eden, the only one, where only your most intimate confidante will get your drift? The scripts keep coming in the strangest forms—the old lady in line at the Los Feliz post office who needs your help to weigh her envelope, or the handsome boy on his bicycle racing down Lincoln Boulevard like a messenger from youth to say all this will continue.

# Hours in Logos

Is this between time, a warp in which eternity occurs, or life itself, these hours when you browse at leisure among the used volumes, cruising the new arrivals with nothing in mind—as if you needed another book—and finding, say, some tales of Tolstoy in an old edition, illustrated, probably from the forties but without a date, for five bucks, so you indulge your lust for the ancient real, if words imprinted on paper before Zip codes existed can be called real in such virtual times. There is music, too, in those rolling racks of discs and in the bins where even LPs linger to be flipped through in search of nothing but the unexpected, that obscure masterpiece you've heard of but never heard, which seems to make it sweeter even if you're missing the machine to play it. There is consolation in the physical, these objects you feel in your fingers as you contemplate their contents, the paradoxically disembodied melodies, the sentences released in your mind as you listen or read. Real sounds, too, serenade you, thanks to the unpredictable tastes of the clerks spinning their preferred music to work by through hidden speakers, sometimes as if speaking to some self of yours you thought lost, yet a few notes and those years have returned and you nod, recognizing the familiar rhythm, intimately remote. And so you remain amid the shelves and the big tables piled with remainders, relishing the uselessness of this pursuit of the permanent mysteriously embodied in these books, inanimate yet surely alive in a way even their authors no longer are. You are among your kind, communing in this curious place to which you return always as to an inn on some long road between towns. These hours are yours alone, when there's nowhere you need to be but here and now, and you are in your element, content simply to swim in these calm waters where all the words in the world, or those whose coolness soothes the soul, slowly swirl and flow.

# On the 101

Doing 80 along the dotted line through the lettuce fields of the Salinas Valley, a cropduster helicopter crossing overhead, and then what's left of the eucalyptus windbreaks shredded by a century of weather, and miles of grapevines tied up in every direction in military precision all the way to the foothills, and after that the rotting barracks of Camp Roberts, who am I to complain about the violations of this landscape, I'm driving a car, sucking the melted dinosaurs out of the earth like the oil derricks nodding near King City, and for the ten-thousandth time I marvel at what remains of the summery gold hills studded with oaks beyond the subdivisions and the shopping malls and the dust clouds plowed up by the food factories. There is still some blue sky between the cities, and compact discs in the dashboard to accompany my gloomy musings, and the Golden Gate stands shining someplace behind me and deeper south the Hollywood Freeway is choked up as ever as at the climax of a romantic movie, only instead of the stars snuggling on screen with swoony music on the soundtrack there are commuters cocooned in their cockpits with audiobooks or talk shows no less degenerate than mine. And so I stake my claim to this inspiring and disgraceful state with its poets subverting the schools, its acidhead techno-entrepreneurs replacing the razed orchards, its historic adobes, its missions long since leveled by time and restored in convincing facsimile, and further north its Luther Burbank Gardens and Frank Lloyd Seuss government centers and shady plazas lined with first-rate tasting rooms, and this long road connecting everything including the big rigs and the RVs, the Honda Civics and the red Ferraris, the Cadillac Escalades and Subaru Foresters and CHP cruisers speeding south and racing north as if there were someplace to go, and maybe there is, as I am rolling all these hours to see my Uncle Henry in Santa Barbara, he's ninety-six and still alive and we are grateful and relieved to know there is a King's Highway that links us across these hundreds of familiar miles.

# Having Sex in Mexico with Cernuda

You died of a heart attack in Coyoacán when I was just sixteen, an age
at which you would have desired my wiry boy's body so much like
yours had been on those Andalusian beaches of your adolescence
when sex came to life in your tanned skin and you found undying
delight in those beautiful other boys' limbs, and mine would have
rhymed with theirs, and though I wasn't gay and was yet to come
in my first love's naked embrace, half a century later I can imagine
how much I might have pleased you in your final months, traveling
back in time and a thousand miles to find you at home in exile, and
driving together to Zihuatanejo for a swim in the warm Pacific
and some fresh fish tacos and a couple of cold Bohemias (though
I would be underage) and then retire to a siesta in our beachfront
hotel bungalow where you would ravish me with your Castilian
Spanish and the tragic wisdom of one who knows that poetry solves
no problems, only accentuates the agonies, intensifies the pleasures
of perpetual loss, caressing my young manhood and initiating me
into the ecstasies and occult mysteries of forbidden love—you
would adore me and my darkness and my lightness as I moved
with you through the Mexican afternoon, receiving transmission of
your genius into my astounded soul by way of the passion surging
between us, all for the sake of your sweet release from years of
lovelessness, and so these decades later I might hold your longing
and make it mine, possessed by your lines like delicious kisses
making me your medium, and in Madrid when you were gone, be
smitten with your handsome face smiling at me from the back of
your book, and since then be enamored of your formal grace on
the page, seduced by your melancholy solitude in equipoise with
mine, and prove more faithful than all your other sun-browned
boys combined, still able to hear your voice and bring you alive in a
tongue you know, even though it isn't yours.

# Too Much, Too Late

Too much music, too many words, too many poems, too much news, too many people, too much noise, excess everything, even the sound of my own voice, sight of my face in the mirror, revealing how much more aged I am than I could ever believe or have a right to be, given all those who were dead by the time they would have been this old, too much death but also too much life, too much to notice and record, celebrate and regret, acknowledge and ignore, swimming in contradictions of my own construction, prisoner of my own compulsions, pushed and driven by some inner demon who believes language will be all that's left when no one is around to read, so even the archived documents, these shredded remnants, will be scattered and settle states apart where refugees will pick through them in search of something to save but they will be mistaken, it will prove too late, too far beyond salvation, redemption, confession, too late for apologies, too little light to read by if there was ever a stray page that escaped the storm, a stray cat that came through unscathed, a wild card that landed in a winning hand, but too much already happened, we are in overtime, way past closing, and the ones who didn't find mates during business hours are out of luck and the ones home writing in their rooms are equally doomed, all going down under the weight of too much stuff to belong to anyone as it swirls through the sky at high speeds leaving grief in its wake and trails of tears and traces of who we thought we were though that has since proved illusory, we are no one but these pieces and shards, slivers of fresh ruins, crash helmets useless, smartphones dumb, there's nobody anywhere to call and no connection, we are on our own and afraid to sleep lest what little we have be taken, but take these riches off my plate, it's full and I can't contain it anymore, I'm spilling everything and it's late but not even midnight.

# Marriott Courtyard, Culver City

From the western windows of Suite 819 you have a long view of the 405 streaming at the limit in both directions on an ordinary Sunday in October. The light has a bright metallic glare, but if you stand close to the glass and look left, south through the haze toward LAX, there is a green expanse that soothes the eye: Hillside Memorial Park, the Jewish cemetery with the statue of Al Jolson atop his tomb in a circle of columns that give the surrounding lawn a center—all the flat gravestones sunk in the grass arranged as if in homage to the entertainer. Amid the agitated landscape of Los Angeles the grassy slopes of Hillside are anomalously calm while the city vibrates with barely contained aggression, even on the Sabbath. I regard the eighth-floor view with wonder because just northwest of Jolson I can see where my parents are buried—my father's ashes first, my mother's later—and of all the hotels in greater LA this is the one where I have come to see Louise, who raised me in my early years while my folks were out making their fortune. Although she quit when I was seven to start her own family, we've never lost touch and now she is ninety and blind, and Bobby, her adopted son, is taking care of her with help from Melanie, his lady friend; Phillip, one of Louise's former foster children, a middle-aged mentally handicapped alcoholic, rounds out the family of four displaced from their home in South LA by a conflagration started by Dominique, another foster child, who was smoking crack last week and burned the house down, just like that—a house where Louise had lived for more than sixty years. It was insured, thank God, though they are cleansed of their possessions and, until the insurance company finds them another house, are camped in this hotel. It could be worse. Although she can't see, Louise is pleased I've come, and of her loss she simply says, "Ain't no use in me complainin' 'cause there ain't nothin' I can do about it anyway."

# Boardwalk Odyssey

You must pass through the purgatory of the cacophony arcade with its blasting approximations of music and blinking machines that eat your tokens in exchange for noise and flashing wheels of colored lights and bulbs without the slightest idea. When you emerge into sunlight the Chinese circus is tumbling across the stage above the beach and spellbound mobs are applauding the acrobats, especially the girl in red silk who does handstands on stacks of chairs as if the cable holding her up were pure air, disbelief suspended in space and time. Boys are throwing baseballs at the same metal milk bottles as always, these games, these rides, these frightful houses haunting eternity with their recurrent hot dogs and fried childhoods, romance of adolescence, eighth-grade girls made up to look like hookers strolling in search of sex when they are, without quite knowing it, sex itself at the dawn of adult regret. Riders of the machines are screaming clamped into their seats by steel bars and you can feel the terror of your first rollercoaster, fear of flying into infinity at Ocean Park in the fifties, your sister and brother powerless to prevent your death, though you have endured and survived these long decades to relive everything several times over, even this bemusement at the parks of summer where the smells of salt and sugar and bubbling oils and lotions coat one's skin with a strange nostalgia, current pleasures complicated by consciousness, memory infecting every moment with its endless vanishings and streams of people and their foreign faces recognized as always in the intimacy of myth. Bronzed and fleeting, ancient as Greece itself, you are again anointed with olive oil and laurels as your glistening limbs smile under the strokes of imagined hands, those of the same girls who tried to seduce Odysseus. The sirens you hear are in your own mind responding to the emergency of remembering everything, just as these refugees hold their phones to photograph moments of escaping play. You and they will return from your journeys tired with tales of perils and wonders beyond your strength to describe.

# Air Cubana

When the captain came on half-way across the Gulf to announce that due to a mechanical problem we were returning to José Martí, I thought that instead of meeting my love in Mexico City I was going to die in the ocean. My seatmate didn't seem concerned, nodding toward the two men a few rows over and identifying them as Argentines, their arrogant body language gave them away. She had struck up a conversation with me before we boarded, had seen me the day before at Casa de las Américas where I'd gone to interview the editor of its magazine and found myself herded into his office with a group of leftist tourists from Seattle, not an ideal situation for asking skeptical questions. Was she interested in me because of my cool, or was she sent to check if I was CIA? Back at the airport while mechanics were fixing the plane, we were fed a free lunch and as many *Cuba libres* as we could drink, so by the time we boarded again I was buzzed and my Spanish more fluent than usual. We had a philosophical conversation with political undertones and I couldn't tell whether she was trying to seduce me or recording what I was saying for her superiors, or both. Such communist intrigue was beside the point, I was just a journalist and I already had a date in DF, so was not available for deeper interrogation. Perhaps someone had trailed me the other day when I had been befriended by three young dissidents in the Plaza de la Revolución, or maybe the interviewer from Radio Habana smelled something counterrevolutionary in my replies to his questions, or some chorus girl at the Tropicana had looked at my long hair and fingered me as gay, when all I wanted was to see my *chilanga,* who was to meet me in the terminal, so when I walked away from my companion she looked at me with a puzzled expression, as if to say, You *yanqui* spies are not even up for sexual adventure—what kind of spy is that?

# Village Vanguard

That slice-of-pie–shaped space two flights down those steep steps beneath Seventh Avenue, the subway rumbling somewhere under that, is where you descended to discover, despite the posts between you and the stage, and the smoke before cigarettes were illegal, and the closeness of the very cool clientele, with the coolest, the musicians, in back by the bar—to unearth the historic music of New York. The players onstage touched their strings and keys and brushed their drums and kissed their horns with casual expertise, and the patrons nodded in proximity to the familiar rhythms, waitresses snaking their way between tables with their little trays of drinks that clinked when set down as if on cue for their subtle percussion, and it felt snug there underground, secure despite the mayhem upstairs, the taxis hurtling, the agitated addicts, the sirens on fire, streaking lights of the streets, bridge-and-tunnel people stalking the West Village on a Friday night. Sipping your drink you were a citizen and if you were accompanied by your love it was a sexy interregnum, and if solo you could imagine anything because the city's multiplicity meant whatever you made of it, if only on paper, and like the soundwaves flooding your senses the ink flowing from your instrument felt like life itself, music and words together mixing an elixir more intoxicating than cocktails. All those hours under the spell of saxophones and nimble fingers waxing pianistic, or around the corner at the Blue Note or at Birdland uptown or Blue Smoke on the East Side, whatever club was allowing you to muse while the players blew and the bartenders did their dances, grew in you to mean even more than they did in the moment, they drenched you in melodies whose meanings you must translate still even though the original sounds are long gone and what you hear now are other virtuosos thousands of miles removed whose notes seem to surge up from subterranean regions, pockets of relief for refugees from the city's dissonant yet strangely appealing racket. How odd to find the heart is healed by such transfusions.

# Wine Country

The land is strapped with endless lines of tightly tended vines, staked and tied in identical postures of bondage for the pleasure of epicures miles and years away who will someday sip their fruit in a restaurant with their wives or some dame they're trying to seduce, row crops crucified near the creek bed, in the flood plain, unnaturally implanted on formerly green or golden hills where grasses smelled wet as rain or dry as summertime as you drove past on a California road. Now the whole state is grapes and they are good for business, winemakers squeezing the last drops out of the tender skins and aging them in oak or stainless steel and in the imaginations of the tasters and sommeliers whose sensitive tongues must discern not just the flavor but the poetry required to describe such subtly various shades of red, of white, of the gleam in your eyes over the rim of your glass when we toast after we've been apart. That's why these liquids exist, like sacred blood, to seal our desire, which transcends flesh as we are aged in these containers that can't contain our spirits, which keep spilling as if forever. We are reminded of each other always by these aromas as we mourn the earth and regret all that we can't drink. How many trees razed add up to how many cases of contentment, how far can we go before there is nothing but wine as far as the eye can cry, because we are crying at the same time as drinking in the landscape we love as we do our bodies in these acts of communion. If wine were fire it would have consumed the forests, the valleys, the cities long since where we sit and sip in the last polite lives we'll have before we are animals again, mating and grazing, hunting and gathering whatever's left after the storms. Here's to our habitat, my love, as it was before being cleared and bound and pressed to get us drunk, and as it will be when civilization is a word in some language nobody can remember.

# From the Front Deck

It's hardly a deck, really, more like a little porch but open to the grayish blue sky and the utility wires like a big spider web over the whole street. So even without a wireless connection you can see a lot, how for example the clouds cool and color the afternoon with their flying slowly changing shapes as in some Joni Mitchell song, and cover the man in his front yard working on what looks from here like a drill press and sounds like a loud woodpecker on coke when he bears down. Not even a car—but there's one—at this hour of a slow Saturday when errands have been run and copies made and peppers brought home from the farmers market and a few groceries picked up while the store was swarming with people and the clerks cheerfully encouraging them to "have a great day" and almost sounding sincere. The potato seller was gossiping to her girlfriend about the boy who asked her if she'd like to see the world from the back of his Harley, and she just laughed. "I'm more of a Honda girl," says her friend, and they both have another little chuckle enjoying the power they wield over desperate men. An ordinary day and yet simmering with significance, even cars in their hard way somehow emanating creation. Gazpacho composed for lunch, a slice or two of fresh bread, the sound of the country band belting out a song in front of the bakery even as the exhaust soot settles steadily over everything are signs of something you can't put your finger on but it leaves its mark in your whorls. Those flocks of tiny specks flying east over the coast almost seem to know where they're going, so quick and straight are their wakes above the composition shingles across the street. You ride your bike but you don't hike or go out of your way to look for things yet find if you sit still they sometimes come to you. It helps if you have an Adirondack chair and can park yourself in the partial sun, clutch your arthritic fingers around a pen and pay attention.

# Sunset Boulevard

It starts downtown then angles through Hollywood before it begins to get sexy past Beverly Hills and curves west all the way through the Palisades to the bay. Kids in fast cars late at night may try to test their skills at high speeds and be surprised by the LAPD or a turn just slightly tighter than they expected so they crash, perhaps for the last time. I could have been one of those but I lucked out. Later my mother lived just around the bend from Norma Desmond. Curves, cars, matriarchs holed up in their haciendas, countless recurrent drives that took you without even a star map across the constellation of Los Angeles, the turf you long since eschewed that stays with you anyway and you can't escape no matter how many miles and years you put between you and its tarry heart, which is entangled blackly and most stickily with yours despite these distances. How the landscape changes, yet the manicured lawns look eternal, brilliantly green as in the fifties, and the sleazy motels farther east also the same only with different drugs, and the taquerías of Silverlake more numerous. Is Bukowski's bungalow on De Longpre a historic stop on the bus tour of famous homes of the broke and drunk? Will my mom's spread ever get its plaque declaring it the site of my showdown with her boyfriend that night when he went back to the Valley to fetch his Luger and I spent sleepless hours awaiting his return to finish me off? I wonder if the avocados are still falling off the big tree in the garden and whether kingfishers are still raiding the koi pond for a beakful of pricey sushi. None of my business, if it ever was, but the mind is drawn electromagnetically along its lines of most resistance to its coldest cases, its forgotten crimes to which it must all but confess. The mystery is never solved, can't be explained away, the clues lead not far enough, yet you can almost reconstruct the drama by tracing the lost steps, the skidmarks, the forensics of whatever's left.

# Dream Museum

It's in a warehouse on the edge of town, or one of those factories now abandoned whose labyrinthine corridors and cold dark stairwells lead to galleries where everything is collected: locks of my lost hair and the hair of those referred to elsewhere in these pages, my whole collection of manual typewriters picked up at yard sales and rustic flea markets, boxes of historic snapshots under glass that illustrate what happened to my family, piles of non-archival newspapers with my writings that slowly yellow and decompose before the reader's eyes, my baseball gloves, the poison pen I killed my mother with in a vain attempt to advance my career, the spell with which I brought her back to life—artifactual evidence of one among countless existences whose stuff has proved more durable than flesh, curated by my unacknowledged children, mostly grown by now, whose job it is to guide tours of my afterlife where you the visitor may imagine how it felt to crash my bike and smash my ancient face on Mesa Lane, or gather those dried-up roses in my prime, or roll that '64 Porsche in the Arizona snow of US 66, or fall in the pool with my cowboy boots and Hopalong Cassidy six-shooters, all of which are on display as you wander in a daze from room to room. My disembodied voice is digitized and recites my complete works on a chip implanted in your head that can be rented at the desk, and in the gift shop all my unsold books, rescued from the boxes in my garage, can be purchased from my heirs whose child support I hope the revenues contribute to. Animatronic miniature models of poets I have known will, for a dollar each, complain about my unrelenting correspondence, with canceled stamps and envelopes as proof of my fruitless campaign to save the postal service, and how my letters annoyed, amused, bemused or inspired them, depending on the mood. A *catalogue dérangé* of 1947 pages accounts for everything you've seen, heard, smelled or tasted—but did not touch—in this ephemeral exhibition it took a lifetime to traverse.

**Stephen Kessler** was born in 1947 in Los Angeles. He attended UCLA, received a BA in languages and literature from Bard College and an MA in literature from the University of California, Santa Cruz. He was a founding editor of the independent literary publishers Green Horse Press and Alcatraz Editions, the international journal *Alcatraz*, and the weekly newspapers the *Santa Cruz Express* and *The Sun*, and has published hundreds of essays, articles, interviews, and reviews in dozens of periodicals, as well as nine books of poetry, sixteen books of literary translation, three collections of essays, and a novel. He is the editor and principal translator of *The Sonnets* by Jorge Luis Borges, and a recipient of the Harold Morton Landon Translation Award from the Academy of American Poets, a National Endowment for the Arts Fellowship, and a Lambda Literary Award for his translations of the Spanish poet Luis Cernuda. He lives in Northern California, where he edited *The Redwood Coast Review* from 1999 through 2014. For more about Stephen Kessler, visit www.stephenkessler.com.